AWAKENING THE LIGHT WARRIOR WITHIN

The journey out of the darkness
and into the light,
taking back your power
and reclaiming your worth.

DAVID JAMES DI PARDO

Copyright © 2019 by David James Di Pardo

Awakening the Light Warrior Within

The journey out of the darkness and into the light, taking back your power and reclaiming your worth.

All rights reserved. No part of this publication may be reproduced, distributed or transmitted in any form or by any means, including photocopying, recording, or other electronic or mechanical methods, without the prior written permission of the author, except in the case of brief quotations embodied in critical reviews and certain other noncommercial uses permitted by copyright law. Neither the author nor the publisher assumes any responsibility or liability whatsoever on behalf of the consumer or reader of this material. Any perceived slight of any individual or organization is purely unintentional. The resources in this book are provided for informational purposes only and should not be used to replace specialized training and professional judgment of a health care or mental health care professional. Neither the author nor the publisher can be held responsible for the information provided within this book. Please always consult a trained professional before making any decisions regarding treatment of yourself or others. Although each of the chapters in this book remain factual, some names have been changed to protect the identity and privacy of individuals and their families.

ISBN: 978-1-9991625-0-4

First Edition

Editor: Kathryn Willms, Proofreading: Michelle Parker

Cover and interior design: David James Di Pardo

An imprint of David James Di Pardo

DavidD.ca

@daviddcoach f 📷 🐦 P

For all inquiries including media, speaking, and bulk purchases please contact info:davidd.ca

DEDICATION

For Lara, my sister, friend, and fellow Warrior. You saw the light in me before I did. Through the ups and downs, you reminded me of that light, even when I was engulfed by darkness and forgot it was there. You recognized my light because it is the same light that exists within you. Throughout all your struggles, you never lost faith, hope, or the ability to love: the three tools of the Warrior. I am a Light Warrior because you showed me how to be one.

Love, D.

CONTENTS

PREFACE 1

THE LONGEST NIGHT 5

CHAPTER 1
A SPARK OF HOPE 13

CHAPTER 2
LETTING GO OF "WHY" 31

CHAPTER 3
AWAKENING COMPASSION 43

CHAPTER 4
RADICAL ACCEPTANCE 55

CHAPTER 5
COURAGE AND HEART WORDS 69

CHAPTER 6
CENTERING, GROUNDING, AND CLARITY 83

CHAPTER 7
FORGIVENESS: FOR YOU, NOT THEM 97

CHAPTER 8
SELF-LOVE: NOT THE SAME AS SELF-CARE 111

CHAPTER 9
WHEN YOU'VE DONE THE WORK 129

CHAPTER 10
EVERY IDEA HAS ITS DAWN 145

CHAPTER 11
FINDING TRUTH 163

CHAPTER 12
LIGHT WARRIOR 179

MANIFESTO OF THE LIGHT WARRIORS 195

ACKNOWLEDGMENTS 201

PREFACE

This book was conceived on June 8th of 2017. It had been over a year since my separation, I was living in a new home, and I had recently taken up writing. I had never thought of myself as a writer before or believed I possessed any discernible skill for communicating via the written word. But, every time I sat down to write, I felt a wave of words rush through me, propelling my fingers across the keyboard. It was as if I was on autopilot and channeling some higher wisdom. That same wave crashed over me on June 8th, a warm summer night, as I stood in the shower. Quickly stepping out of the shower and drying my hands, I reached for my phone to start transcribing the words in my head, knowing that I may lose them if I didn't. At first, they seemed like an indiscernible mishmash. Then I took a second look.

Radical Acceptance
Letting Go of Why
The Spark of Hope
Awakening Compassion
Finding Truth

I knew then that I had been given the chapters for this book and a rough framework to build around. For a while, I had felt like I had a book inside of me, but I had no idea where to start. Now I did. Over the summer months of 2017, I sat down to write this book on multiple occasions, rewriting the first three chapters more times than I care to admit. But the pages and words were filled with so much anger and pain that, each time, I had to stop myself. I was compelled to write about my marriage and relationships, their darkest moments and challenges, but I struggled to find a way to share my story and my truth without exposing or assuming the truth of others, and still creating something that would serve a purpose in this world. So, I reached out to my mentors for support and guidance. Their advice was unanimous: Stop writing.

They told me that I had to take the time to finish healing, release my judgment of others, and complete the cycle of forgiveness before I could share my story and serve others. I was reluctant to heed their advice; I felt I had already done the work. But they were right. I spent the next year not writing but healing what was left of my broken heart. Through that process emerged the same book but with a different purpose. It became less about sharing my story and more about sharing the tools and practices that I had learned throughout my journey. The practices that had contributed to my healing and flooded my life with light and purpose.

This book is a hybrid, part memoir and part self-help, chronicling the hardest decade of my life. There is still darkness and pain sprinkled throughout its pages because, until we acknowledge the darkness, we cannot bring in the light. This book is an invitation to become a Light Warrior, to walk the path of light that shines on the darkness to dissolve the fears and hatred that pollute our world and lives. I like the term "warrior" because this journey requires action, putting in the work, and holding the line when life would try and push us back to where we started. Tempting us to resort to our old ways of being. The time for passivity is over. Taking back your power requires the acknowledgment that you gave it away. Reclaiming your worth requires deeply knowing that it's inherent and you never walked a single step without it.

Each chapter of this book is filled with personal anecdotes, and bits and pieces of my story, followed by a section called

#LightTalk. This is where I get real about what I learned through my journey and provide practices to dispel the heaviness and bring in more light into your life. Throughout these sections, I will share the meditations, practices, and exercises that guided me on my journey and helped me emerge from the darkness.

BUT FIRST, WHO ARE THE LIGHT WARRIORS?

When I embarked on my journey towards personal and spiritual growth, I came across the term Lightworker. Lightworkers are those who devote their time and energy to being a beacon of light in the world. Looking to make it a better place. But to me, we need to be more than just devoted to light and to ourselves. Devotion isn't enough—we live in a world where action is required to effect real change and spread more light. Hence the term Light Warrior was born. Light, here, is synonymous with love, trust, faith, connection, compassion, etc. *A Course In Miracles* defines light as the divine essence within us but not of us. It is what contributes to our shared humanity and connects us to our brothers and sisters. I love both definitions because I consider them to be one and the same. When we allow our light to shine, when we embrace all of who we are, we allow others to recognize the light that is within them. The light that guides them on their path. With social and political systems crumbling, we constantly face injustices and separations based on race, gender, religion, and sexual orientation. Every day we must fight for truth, for equality, for love, for animal welfare, for our planet, for the well-being of our brothers and sisters. We can be the voices for those who have none. The voices of those who are afraid to speak and who have been beaten down by life. And so, we are more than lightworkers;

we seek light, embody it, spread it, and fight for it. We are warriors. We are Light Warriors.

Our journey into the light requires that we first navigate our way through the darkness. We must remove the blindfold we have placed over our eyes and, in some cases, see for the very first time. Awakening to what was within us all along.

To our journey together.
Love,
David

THE LONGEST NIGHT

It was a late February evening in 2012. I was home alone while my then-husband was out with a friend. We had been married for five years at this point; in fact, it was the anniversary of our first date. I had come home after a long day at work, put on my pajamas, and was now opening the mail.

Opening mail never fails to stress me out, a holdover from the days when the envelopes were full of letters from collectors and past due notices. I hadn't started off with much and had put myself through design school by taking out government and bank loans, and by working part-time. After graduating, I had done contract work for a couple of years. We had married when I was 21 and bought a condo using our honeymoon funds as a down payment. Between our mortgage, loan payments, and bills, it was tough to make ends meet. Eventually, I had gotten a job in the manufacturing industry. It wasn't my passion (at least not yet), but it eased our financial pressures. While money still wasn't abundant, the days of stressing over bills were behind us. And yet somehow opening mail instantly put knots in my stomach and caused my muscles to tense. I wondered if that would ever go away.

So I was already in an anxious state when I came across the envelope from the electric company. You know the ones: the logo is the same but the envelope is different, and you instantly know this isn't your typical monthly statement. I took a deep breath and ripped it open. Final Notice. Our account was months past due and, if the amount wasn't paid in full, services would be disconnected in 10 days. I felt waves of red-hot anger rush over me. I scanned the letter quickly, but the past due amount was nowhere to be found. I picked up the phone to unload on my husband. He had taken over the finances a few years back because dealing with them gave me such terrible anxiety. Since then, the invoices had been emailed directly to him so I didn't have to see them, one of the benefits of going green. But now the system had failed. When my husband answered, I let him have it. He tried to calm me down, but I was incredibly annoyed. I hung up the phone, with a "fine, I'll do everything myself" attitude.

I reached for his tablet to find our statement of account among his emails. I scrolled through a few messages and then I stopped dead in my tracks. It wasn't our electric bill, but an electronic invoice for a delivery of flowers, red roses to be exact. Only, I hadn't received any flowers. As I looked over the invoice, I learned they had been sent to another man, one who lived in Mexico. I didn't recognize the name; it wasn't one I had heard before. Instructions had been given for the inclusion of a special note to accompany the flowers; it was in Spanish and, loosely translated, read, "You are the owner of my heart. I will fight for you." I could feel my heart pounding in my chest. My mind instantly became confused as if a fog had rolled in. I must be mistaken. I was missing something, some element that would cause all of this to make sense, so we could laugh about it later. I dug deeper, looking for rational explanations.

The more I dug, the worse it got: the lies were bigger than I had imagined. There had been other betrayals and violations of trust over the past five years of marriage, but nothing like this. As my rage subsided, it was replaced by shock. They had met eight months prior while my husband was in Mexico for a wedding. The night had been spent talking in the hotel lobby, and later up in the mystery man's hotel room. I logged on to social media to try and get some answers about who this mystery man was. On his Instagram, I found pictures showing the roses and love note he had received from my husband, the ones for which I had just found the receipt. I also found evidence of text exchanges, ranging from love notes and emotional confiding to daily messages wishing each other good morning and good night. They had been sending each other gifts through the mail, which explained the new items that had been popping up around the house, which my husband had explained away as gifts from friends.

I felt stupid and ashamed. The person I married and trusted wholeheartedly no longer existed. The man I had given my heart to, and shared my deepest wounds with, vanished in an instant and everything I had previously known in my heart to be true was placed into question. Suddenly, I was married to a stranger. I thought about packing a bag, taking the dogs, and leaving for my parents' house, but I didn't. I was too ashamed. I couldn't face the reality of the situation, let alone try and explain it to someone else. My mind raced as I considered the implications of this betrayal. I had just signed a sales contract to buy a new house, and our realtor was in the process of listing our condo on the market and lining up visits with potential buyers. I reached for the phone—not to call a friend, because who would understand?—but to call my husband again. He answered, sounding frustrated that I had interrupted his evening for a second time, but as soon as I spoke and he heard the waver in my voice, he fell silent. I summoned every last bit of strength I had and demanded he come home immediately. He did.

Thus began the longest night of my life. Our relationship had been shattered, or at least my perception of it had been. But it wasn't over yet. I would spend the next five years trying to glue the pieces of our marriage back together. In the years leading up to my divorce, as well as for some time following it, I would hit rock bottom over and over again. Over time, rock bottom would start to feel like a comfortable space. Because as long as I stayed down, things couldn't get much worse. I would come to lose everything, myself included, but through the journey find something more powerful that turned out to be all my heart had ever longed for. This is the Light Warrior's journey.

WE ARE POWERLESS TO CHANGE

WHAT
WE
DON'T
ACCEPT.

CHAPTER 1

A SPARK OF HOPE

OWNING OUR STORY CAN BE HARD BUT NOT NEARLY AS DIFFICULT AS SPENDING OUR LIVES RUNNING FROM IT. EMBRACING OUR VULNERABILITIES IS RISKY BUT NOT NEARLY AS DANGEROUS AS GIVING UP ON LOVE AND BELONGING AND JOY—THE EXPERIENCES THAT MAKE US THE MOST VULNERABLE. ONLY WHEN WE ARE BRAVE ENOUGH TO EXPLORE THE DARKNESS WILL WE DISCOVER THE INFINITE POWER OF OUR LIGHT.

— BRENÉ BROWN, *THE GIFTS OF IMPERFECTION: LET GO OF WHO YOU THINK YOU'RE SUPPOSED TO BE AND EMBRACE WHO YOU ARE*

SHATTERED TRUST

Learning to trust again is some of the hardest work we'll ever do. For some of us, we will spend a lifetime rebuilding it with people who have hurt or betrayed us, to heal wounds that run deep. Trust cannot be measured or secured; there is no way to ensure it has been achieved and won't be compromised again. Building and maintaining trust is an ongoing process that requires continuous effort and deliberate thought.

Brené Brown, PhD, is a shame researcher, New York

Times best-selling author, and speaker whose TED Talks are among the most-viewed inspirational talks on the Internet. She speaks about trust as a jar of marbles. Small actions and moments add marbles to the jar, while moments of missed connection—because we don't have the time or take the time—take marbles out. When we see someone we know or love is in pain or distress, and we choose to continue moving through our day without taking a moment to establish connection and listen or provide a shoulder to lean on, we break trust. When we notice someone react to something we have said or done, but decide not to acknowledge it or verify if our words or intentions have been misperceived, we break trust. These moments can add and subtract marbles from our trust jars.

My husband hadn't just removed some marbles from our jar of trust; he had blown the whole damn jar to pieces. Now there were shards of glass and marbles everywhere, and there I was, tippy-toeing through the mess, too busy to find a new jar, unsure if I wanted to start collecting marbles again. It felt like my life was a piñata and someone had taken a baseball bat to it. No, not just "someone": the person I loved.

I was reluctant to move forward with the purchase of the house. But, in the hours and days following the implosion of our relationship and the shattering of my trust, he begged and pleaded with me not to cancel the purchase. This marked a huge shift. He had previously been reluctant to leave the city and buy a house in the suburbs, but I had pushed for it. I had wanted a house with a great big yard where the dogs and our future kids would run around and play, and a garden, surrounded by a white picket fence, where I would grow fresh herbs and organic vegetables. Cliché, I know. Adopting kids had always been the plan, but now it was the furthest thing from my mind. I told myself buying the house would at least give the dogs more room, and maybe I could still grow some healthy produce, but I was on the fence. The future had never seemed more uncertain; thinking about what it might bring scared me more than I could express.

Meanwhile, my husband was searching desperately for even the smallest strand of hope. The new house, which he had previously described as a cage confining him and keeping him from living in the city, was now his shot at salvation—and a fresh start. He pleaded and begged, and eventually the compassionate—and overly tolerant—side of me gave in. Contracts were signed and checks were cut. It was a decision I would regret sooner than I could imagine.

Once we committed to buying the house, we had to sell the condo quickly. Night after night, potential buyers came by to see the place. Each visit required us to clean the house all over again... because dogs. Then we had to be careful to make sure nothing was moved out of place. It felt like we were guests in our own home. I'd arrive home from work and scramble to quickly walk the dogs, tidy up, and leave before the visitors arrived. Usually I would take refuge in my car along with the dogs, parked on the street a few yards away so that barking dogs wouldn't upset the viewing. I was still extremely hesitant about the path I had chosen, but part of me couldn't wait to sell the condo and leave. The place I had once loved was now tainted and filled with painful memories. The spot where I was standing when I found out. The corner where I sat crying, my face buried in my knees. Heart-wrenching memories, everywhere I looked.

As we waited for the condo to sell, issues in our relationship continued to surface and new betrayals transpired. My husband resumed his conversations with the mystery man from Mexico. He argued that it was because he had no one here—he had immigrated a year prior to us meeting, and his family and childhood friends lived in a different country—but the messages being exchanged were beyond friendly. This man received words and love notes I had never been worthy of. Our confrontations would result in him making promises that were soon broken, causing me fresh bouts of agony. Down I spiraled each time, further into the darkness. The weekend after Easter, I discovered messages between them talking about how sexy the mystery man looked in his new navy briefs and how navy blue was my husband's favorite color. Navy blue? That was news to me. But of course my despair wasn't about my husband's new favorite color but about the nature of their once-again inappropriate conversations and the fact that they had reconnected despite my husband promising that the relationship had ended. I found myself crying on the kitchen floor, surrounded by a half-drunk bottle of vodka and an unopened bottle of pills. Dramatic, I know, but I was desperate. I didn't want to die; I just wanted the pain to stop.

I was home alone, again. He was out with friends celebrating the arrival of a childhood friend from out of town. In my despair, I reached for the phone and begged him to return home. I couldn't go on and was ready to say my goodbyes. His friends dismissed it as me being overly dramatic and encouraged him to stay. He did.

I sat there on the cold ceramic tile, on the edge, my soul aching. And I prayed. I prayed to God, the Goddess, the Universe, my guardian angels, and just about any other higher power that might be listening. And, well, this isn't one of those stories where a divine light came down to heal my wounds or show me the way, but I did feel something. A wave of warmth and stillness surrounded me, and the world no longer felt like it was spinning. I felt held. And in that moment, that was enough—enough to get me through to another day. I took the dogs and made my way up to bed, leaving some of my pain and loneliness there on the kitchen floor that night. I knew there would be more where that had come from.

THE LETTER

> SO EVEN IF THE HOT LONELINESS IS THERE, AND FOR 1.6 SECONDS WE SIT WITH THAT RESTLESSNESS WHEN YESTERDAY WE COULDN'T SIT FOR EVEN ONE, THAT'S THE JOURNEY OF THE WARRIOR.
> —PEMA CHÖDRÖN, *WHEN THINGS FALL APART: HEART ADVICE FOR HARD TIMES*

The days that followed brought a sliver of light. Finally, there was an offer on our condo. It was significantly lower than what we had hoped for but, desperate to escape, we accepted. Things moved quickly from there. There were documents to sign, the new house to inspect, and a condo to empty. We needed to be out in three weeks so the new owner could take possession. The busyness was good; it kept me distracted.

One afternoon, I called my husband from the office suggesting that we go out for dinner. I figured the change of scenery would do us some good, especially with our move coming up in just a couple of weeks. He didn't think it was a good idea. He ended the call, saying he was busy at work and we would talk that evening. Saying we would talk later didn't seem like a good sign, but how much worse could things possibly get? That night I arrived home first, as usual, and leashed one of the dogs to take her down to the park for her walk. As I left our building, I spotted my husband walking home from the subway stop a few blocks away. As our eyes locked, he turned and began walking in the opposite direction. A few moments later, I received a text message on my phone, instructing me to check my email. I went back upstairs, unleashed the dog, and fetched my tablet, with knots building up in my stomach. There it was, a letter from my husband telling me he was leaving me. He wrote that he had been deeply unhappy for a while, and that the little things that he said didn't bother him, like me adopting a vegan diet, actually did, and he couldn't live like this anymore. He wouldn't be moving to the new house, and our marriage was over. As I sat there waiting for him to arrive home, rage and hysteria set in. I wouldn't be able to take possession of the new house on my own, and I couldn't stay in the condo as we had signed off on the sale the week prior. If he went through with this, I would be homeless.

When he arrived home, we sat down to speak. He insisted his decision didn't have anything to do with the man in Mexico. He was just unhappy, and he had never liked the idea of leaving the city and moving to the suburbs. He was only doing it to make me happy. I couldn't believe it. He had begged me to proceed with the sale. I had heard enough. As tears ran down my face, I grabbed my coat and the dog and told him I was leaving. In response, he grabbed me by the shoulders and pinned me against the wall, stating that he wouldn't let me leave in this condition. I could no longer contain the rage within me; I erupted, pushing him off me and into one of the dining room chairs and punching his arm so hard that bruises would emerge the next day. I had never acted violently to another person before, and I would carry the shame of that act with me for years, and he would remind me of it relentlessly. At that moment I vowed to never raise my hand towards another being again.

Tears flooded our faces and it was hours before we could speak. When words finally came, we made an agreement. If the problem truly was leaving the city and moving to the suburbs, we would try it on a conditional basis. If, after a year, he still wasn't happy there, I promised we would sell and move back to the city. I knew the city was not where I envisioned my future or starting a family, but I was willing to make the sacrifice if it meant saving my marriage.

And so the move proceeded, and within a week I was painting the new house while my husband finished the packing.

Moving and setting up a new home provided lots of opportunities for busy-making projects, for which I was thankful. Whenever things started to settle down and I had too much time to think, pain and sadness would instantly start to overwhelm me. Staying busy kept me from drowning. But it quickly became clear that escaping the city hadn't brought a new start, or allowed me to escape my problems. They had followed me and, every time I started to collect the marbles off the floor and rebuild my trust, the jar was shattered yet again.

In the months that followed, we would replay the same fights over and over again as he ended and resumed his relationship with the man in Mexico several times. Each time, I would ride a rollercoaster of emotions. Relegating myself to the couch, watching Netflix, avoiding food, and telling family and friends that I was sick in order to get out of social commitments. Sleeping away hours and days on the couch in the basement until I felt strong enough to rejoin the world. Riding out waves of anxiety and panic that would shake my bones, causing my entire body to tremble.

My heart and mind couldn't fathom why he wouldn't

make our relationship and regaining my trust a priority. Instead, he seemed determined to defy and hurt me whenever he could.

Through it all, I told no one. I canceled family engagements and holiday gatherings. I felt like I no longer knew how to be around other people. Part of me was scared to share what I had been living through out of the fear that, if we could somehow save our marriage, they would never be able to look at him the same way again. Ultimately, I suffered in silence and solitude because I didn't think anyone would understand.

A year after we moved into the house, things hadn't gotten better. I needed help—and hope. And then—fortunately, miraculously, thankfully—I found it.

THE SPARK

It's said that God provides the solution to a problem the moment the problem arises. But that doesn't always mean we can see it right away—or, in my case, that I was ready to face and accept it. But when I was, I found that I had been sent more than a solution—I had been sent an angel.

In 2006, a few months before I met my husband, I had met a beautiful woman while working in the tourism industry. She was that rare type of soul, as beautiful and radiant on the inside as on the outside. Our lives had taken unexpected turns and we had both left the tourism industry within six months of each other, but by then a bond had been formed. Since then, our lives had taken completely different paths, but she had become one of my most cherished friends; I called her my "soul sister." She had been the maid of honor at my wedding, helping me enter a new stage of my life. Now, engulfed in pain and sadness, unable to move forward,

I called on her again.

By a weird twist of fate, Lara, my soul sister, had embarked on a new career path as a life coach and was in the process of completing her three-year NLP (Neuro-Linguistic Programming) certification. She was just starting to see clients.

I raised my hand.

So there we sat, face to face in our Ikea chairs, a box of tissues on the table between us, in the spare room of her then-apartment in a beautiful building, formerly a convent, located in downtown Montreal. How fitting, I thought. Here I was, a person who had lost touch with his soul, in a place where people had previously gone to honor theirs. Even the mass-produced chairs felt right. My husband and I had met online, on a popular dating site, responsible for mass-producing connections. We had built a relationship out of fake profiles and a dial-up connection. My husband had lied about his age on his profile, and it wasn't until months after our engagement that the truth had come to light. Just like the chairs, some assembly (and disassembling) had been required.

We talked for what seemed like hours. Coaching came naturally to Lara, almost as if she had been built for it. She had the kind of wisdom that came from having trekked through the trenches of life, tended to her wounds, and gone on to fight another day. She radiated light, the same light that had drawn me to her years prior when we would sit in her office and chat with our morning coffees in hand.

Even in this safe space, I struggled to find words and make sense of everything that had happened. I had been in pain for so long that the pain had become comfortable; sure, it still ached, but it also felt normal. Moving through it seemed like it would only hurt more. Like when you hold your arm in a folded position for too long and the muscles contract, making it ridiculously painful to regain normal movement. I found myself rambling on about insignificant issues until I noticed Lara giving me a look of confusion mixed with gentle compassion. I stopped talking.

"Where have you gone?" she asked me. Because the person sitting in front of her was unrecognizable. Where was the David she had met in years past, the one who was full of life, deeply passionate, and overflowing with ambition? The man who wouldn't take no for an answer and always found a way to bring his dreams to life. Where had he gone?

I sat there contemplating her question. Where had he gone? I knew where he had gone. I had spent every day of the past six years making him smaller and smaller. Afraid that he took up too much room. Diminishing his light a little more every day.

I fumbled my way through my answer. I told her I was afraid. I was afraid that if I embraced all I was, I'd end up alone. What if I took up so much space that there wasn't room in my life for the people I loved? What if they left? How would that be better?

She smiled and gave me a look. After so many years, I knew her looks. It was the look you give a child when you realize their fear is completely ridiculous: half smile, half "are you freakin' serious?" raised eyebrow, and completely tender.

OUR DEEPEST FEAR IS NOT THAT WE ARE INADEQUATE. OUR DEEPEST FEAR IS THAT WE ARE POWERFUL BEYOND MEASURE. IT IS OUR LIGHT, NOT OUR DARKNESS THAT MOST FRIGHTENS US. [...] YOUR PLAYING SMALL DOES NOT SERVE THE WORLD. THERE IS NOTHING ENLIGHTENED ABOUT SHRINKING SO THAT OTHER PEOPLE WON'T FEEL INSECURE

AROUND YOU. [...] AS WE LET OUR OWN LIGHT SHINE, WE UNCONSCIOUSLY GIVE OTHER PEOPLE PERMISSION TO DO THE SAME. AS WE ARE LIBERATED FROM OUR OWN FEAR, OUR PRESENCE AUTOMATICALLY LIBERATES OTHERS.
—MARIANNE WILLIAMSON, *A RETURN TO LOVE: REFLECTIONS ON THE PRINCIPLES OF "A COURSE IN MIRACLES"*

Lara and I had both read *The Secret*, the best-selling book by Rhonda Byrne published in 2006. It introduced the Law of Attraction, which was just becoming mainstream around that time. The Law of Attraction is based on the notion that our thoughts are energy and posits that we attract into our lives the things we most think about. So, a positive mindset and outlook attracts more positive things into our lives, and negativity attracts more negative things. Lara explained that embracing my light would only attract more light and beauty to my life. That my fear was based on one of my limiting beliefs and that it was ok to let myself shine. I heard her words, and I filed them away.

We meditated together, and I could see the life I was living floating away from me in one direction on a small boat—a canoe actually. And in the opposite direction I saw the vision of what I wanted on the horizon. A beautiful family, a loving relationship, a child propped up on my hip. But I clenched my fist, and I pulled back. I wasn't ready to let go of my marriage; I didn't think there was any other path to the family and future I wanted for myself. And truthfully, I worried that if I ended my marriage, I wouldn't find someone else who would love and accept me for who I was. I felt like my best years were behind me, and my husband's infidelity—both physical and emotional—had me believing that I was deeply flawed and unlovable.

But a seed had been planted. A spark of hope had been ignited, whether I realized it or not.

#LIGHTTALK

Primitive cultures and tribes had initiations and rites of passage where boys became men, and girls became women. These practices were based on the idea that trials make us stronger, wiser, and more resilient. It's often said that adversity builds character. I don't believe this to be true: it doesn't build character, it reveals it. Adversity and the trials and challenges in our lives help us strip back the layers, shed the baggage we have been carrying, and remove the masks we've become used to wearing, bringing us closer to our true selves. It can be useful to think of the tragedies and hardships in our lives as initiations to our path and journey. Only, in this case, the path does not lead to adulthood. It is the path of the Light Warrior who brings light into their lives and consequently into the lives of the people around them.

However far along you are on your journey to becoming a Light Warrior, take a moment now to recognize where you are. Recognize not only where you want to go, but also just how far you've come. The path you've walked has led you to this moment, and it isn't without purpose. The darkest nights prepare us for the brightest mornings. Start by honoring where you are, no matter how bleak things may seem. These difficult moments and trials are preparing you, strengthening you, so you can step into something greater. To deny where we are in our lives and on our journey only keeps us trapped in the darkness. We are powerless to change what we don't accept.

Whether you're ready to make a change or just starting to

open yourself up to the idea, the first step involves taking inventory of your life, acknowledging what's not working (naming it if you can), and reaching out for help if you're ready.

There is a big difference between reaching out for help and making a commitment to change. As unhappy as I was with my life, and as much as I knew things needed to change, in my heart, I wasn't ready. I didn't feel like I had done all I could. I hadn't hit my bottom.

The worst was yet to come, but my meeting with Lara confirmed something important. I wasn't alone. I had Lara but, more fundamentally, I had faith. A faith in something greater than myself, despite my inability to name it, and in a better tomorrow. Not all the time, not even every day. Some days it was nowhere to be found. But when I needed it most, it enveloped me, surrounding me with the right people and right circumstances. Despite my loneliness and mounting desperation, my faith kept me held. And even though I wasn't yet willing to make a change, a spark had been ignited. And that's all it takes to light a roaring fire, a single spark. You may find yourself ready to reach out and ask for help, just as you may find yourself suddenly in the presence of those friends, teachers, guides, and mentors who are there to assist. When the student is ready, the teacher will appear. Sometimes our hearts know we are ready before our minds do and attract into our lives an arsenal of tools and fellow Warriors to help us on our journey.

One of those tools, whose teachings and principles I rely on heavily in my own practice and in this book, was a self-study program called *A Course In Miracles*. I first came across *A Course In Miracles* through the work of Gabrielle Bernstein and Marianne Williamson. Despite its name, it isn't a religious practice but a manual and workbook on the principles of psychotherapy and how we can dismantle beliefs systems that don't serve us, allowing for a shift in our perception—the "miracle" referred to in the title.

A Course In Miracles teaches that prayer is the medium for miracles. I've found that to be true. No prayers go unanswered, but the answers don't always come in the form we expect or even desire. Sometimes, the solutions we think we want don't actually serve or contribute to the well-being or betterment of ourselves or others. We can become so attached to the shape and form our solution "should" take that we deny any option that doesn't coincide with what we have envisioned. This can blind us to just how detrimental our envisioned solution may actually be and close us off to the possibility that there may be a better way. And so, we reject and ignore what's right in front of us. The journey continues when we are willing to ask for what we need, even if that is just help, and are ready to receive it. Even if we are not yet willing or ready to act on what we receive, opening the doors to the possibilities of a better life will often be enough to gently pull us forward, no matter how slow or hesitant we may be to walk those initial steps. Leading to a glimpse of the light that lies ahead. So, I encourage you to develop a prayer practice. Pray to whoever resonates with you, be it God, angels, your higher self, your ancestors, or just the ever-expanding Universe. Close your eyes, get honest about where you are and what isn't working, and ask to be guided. Ask for a solution that will be of the highest good for all.

Each of us has a spark that lies within. It goes by many names. Some connect it to divinity and consider it a fragment of, or a tether to, our Creator; others think of it as star matter or the Universe. I simply call it Love—all-encompassing and expanding Love. This divine spark cannot be extinguished, no matter how deep we bury it within us. While in the darkest of times, it may feel like that spark has dimmed into a slow-burning ember, but always remember that the slightest embers, when fanned, can become a roaring flame. No matter how bleak things may seem or how badly life may have burned us, those embers, buried deep within us, are still lit, glowing ever so gently. All we need is for someone to gently blow. The warriors and guides that come into our lives will recognize the light that gently glows within us, and they will teach us to tend to the fire that burns deep within. Even if all we have left is a single ember, that's enough.

LESSONS KEEP COMING UNTIL WE RECOGNIZE

THE
DARKNESS
AND BRING
IT TO THE
LIGHT.

CHAPTER 2

LETTING GO OF "WHY"

> THERE ARE MOMENTS WHEN TROUBLES ENTER OUR LIVES AND WE CAN DO NOTHING TO AVOID THEM. BUT THEY ARE THERE FOR A REASON. ONLY WHEN WE HAVE OVERCOME THEM WILL WE UNDERSTAND WHY THEY WERE THERE.
>
> —PAULO COELHO, *THE FIFTH MOUNTAIN*

OBSESSION & THE RECKONING IT BRINGS

In the months that followed, I searched for answers. I wanted to know "why." Why had my marriage fallen apart? Why had my husband deliberately broken my trust, repeatedly? Why wasn't he making a bigger effort to fix things? Why was everything hanging by a thread?

If you've ever been betrayed or had your trust shattered, you have likely grappled with this intense longing to understand. If you have had to deal with adultery, no matter what form it took, you will know how insidious and damaging this line of questioning can become. Was the other person younger, thinner, prettier, smarter? Why was I not enough? I fell into the trap of thinking that if I could understand why things had fallen apart, it would somehow justify actions that couldn't be justified. My ego tricked me into believing that knowing "why" would take away the hurt. Perhaps it would be my salvation, I naively thought.

My longing for answers quickly morphed into an obsession. Stalking people on Facebook, opening fake profiles, spending hours scouring the internet late into the night.

Off-line, I rifled through pockets and drawers, looking for any thread of evidence that might illuminate the reasons behind my husband's actions. I relentlessly probed my husband with questions, trying to dive deeper and deeper into a topic that no one really wanted to talk about. I had made it my life's purpose to uncover how this had happened to me—and how I was ultimately the one to blame.

WHAT YOU SEEK, YOU SHALL FIND

Fair warning to fellow seekers: what you seek, you shall find.

I spent hours searching for threads of evidence that I wasn't worthy of love or respect, and I found them. I took that evidence and used it to build a case against myself. I satisfied my ego, proving that I had brought this all on myself, except my ego had lied. I didn't feel better; my pain had not subsided. Somehow it had deepened.

I found all the answers that I had hoped weren't true. The mystery man with the flowers, he turned out to be everything I feared. Younger, thinner, more attractive, with a far more lavish lifestyle than mine. At least, that's how it appeared to me; my perception had been twisted to the point that I had lost any objectivity.

The answers I found brought no relief. They weren't really answers at all; just my own interpretations of the "evidence" I had collected. I had found crumbs and smooshed them together until they resembled something relatively whole and discernable. But I hadn't uncovered some truth; I had just created a story to tell myself. The reality was there was no justifiable answer. My husband couldn't tell me why he had been unfaithful because he didn't know. His awareness wasn't broad enough to contemplate what he had done.

A war raged on within me. On one shoulder sat the devil—my ego—which would list all the reasons why I had brought this on myself. On the other shoulder, an angel—my light—would argue back, "No, I was a good person and no one deserves to be mistreated or taken advantage of." Most days, my ego won. My fear continued to drown out my light. Because I had set out on a quest looking for the reasons why this had been my fault, I believed them when I found them. I believed them all.

For a while, I thought that I could wait out my husband's affair and tried to write it off as a chance encounter. They lived worlds apart and would most likely never see each other again. This would eventually fade, right? In the coming months and years, I would come to understand how misplaced this hope was but, even in the present moment, it did nothing to ease my pain or end the struggle within.

Lara became my sounding board. She was still the only person in my life who knew anything about my husband's infidelity. We continued to work through NLP coaching sessions, trying to uncover the truth and bring back the light, but I felt broken and completely disconnected from the person I once was. All I could see was darkness, unaware that I was the one blocking out the light. The one with his hands over his eyes.

Gradually it became clear. I had to abandon my quest for answers. I had backed myself into a corner, and I had no other options now but to step forward.

It was a struggle. I relapsed many times, spiraling downwards each time. Some days I bounced back fast, others it was a slow crawl. I looked for projects and things in my life that lit me up. With so much darkness surrounding me, I took whatever rays of light I could find. In my working sessions with my health coach (yes, I had one of those too), we shifted the focus of our discussions about the future away from my vision of having a family and back onto myself. Who did I want to be? Who could I be? I knew I wanted to be of service somehow, although I had no idea how that would come to pass. But it was there, at the back of my mind. From my adolescent years to the present moment, my life had been filled with so many trials, so much adversity, and so much pain. I told myself it needed to somehow serve a higher purpose. All this pain needed to be for something. I wanted to use what I had learned to help others and shorten their learning curve. Perhaps I could ease some of their pain and shoulder some of their burdens.

I went back to the gym and took up training. The hours pounding weights and pushing through spin classes became my salvation—my therapy sessions—and proved a temporary escape from pain and internal turmoil. There is something to be said of a body at peace. Bodies at peace make peace.

And, while I hadn't fixed the problems in my marriage, I had calmed the waters. Mostly by spending less time at home antagonizing my husband and focusing on his indiscretion. My shift in focus had provided both of us with a moment to catch our breath. The temporary moments of relief I experienced allowed more light in but, little did I know, a storm was brewing.

The truth was nothing had been healed; trust hadn't been repaired. My life was still in pieces. In an effort to subdue the pain further, I looked for more relief. Training became my new fixation. I spent my mornings and evenings in the gym, six days a week, upwards of three hours a day. I made sure there wasn't time to experience pain and, in doing so, replaced one obsession with another. Quietly, at the back of my mind, my ego whispered, "Perhaps if I lost some weight (or a lot of weight), my husband would love me again."

In my warped state of mind, I thought that, to save my marriage, I had to be better. And I equated being healthy, and ultimately thin, with being better. These were the answers I had found and convinced myself were the root of the infidelity in my marriage. I wanted to be everything I thought I wasn't. Everything that had caused my husband to stray. While I trained and made a concerted effort to be fit, he sat on the couch watching reruns and eating Doritos. We all numb ourselves in different ways. The lack of effort he made to take care of himself was a constant reminder of the lack of effort he made to work at our marriage.

Before I knew it, I was back where I started. Looking for answers, probing for "why."

They say that anger comes from our avoidance of pain. I had tried to avoid my pain, but it hadn't gone away. I was starting to rage.

TOLERANCE FOR PAIN MAY BE HIGH, BUT IT IS NOT WITHOUT LIMIT. EVENTUALLY, EVERYONE BEGINS TO RECOGNIZE, HOWEVER DIMLY, THAT THERE MUST BE A BETTER WAY.
—*A COURSE IN MIRACLES*

Except this wasn't the first time there had been something fundamentally wrong with my marriage. A year prior to the infidelity, I had discovered that my husband was active on gay dating sites. Not the one we had met through. These were new profiles, featuring selfies taken in the setting of our then home. This wasn't the first time I had faced infidelity in a romantic relationship. The relationship prior to my marriage had ended for precisely that reason. This realization further spurred my need for answers. If this pattern was repeating itself, was it because there was truly something wrong with me? My ego tried to convince me that was the case. After all the work I had done on myself, here I still was: no change to my relationship or my husband's behaviors. The question of "why" came back to the forefront of my mind. If all the work I had done to make myself a better and more attractive person, which I realized was rather subjective, hadn't changed my circumstances, then what would? Why was I continuously reliving the same patterns and cycles?

A Course In Miracles, as well as most spiritual practices, teaches that lessons keep coming around until the lesson has been learned. They repeat themselves in relationships and encounters of every type until we are ready to look at the darkness and bring it to the light. As time passed, I began to wonder if perhaps there was something deeper that needed to be healed. If these circumstances weren't a result of my appearance, desirability, or weight, something bigger must be at play. The search for answers had become exhausting and, in a way, it had become a numbing device. Because as long as I was busy searching and obsessing, I wasn't feeling. I wasn't fully opening myself up to the magnitude of the pain I was immersed in for fear that it would drown me. But I realized there were no detours or shortcuts. The only way to surpass the pain would be to move through it and allow myself to feel every heart-wrenching ache. I had to let the tears flow until they had all been cried and not a single tear remained. Opening myself up to the pain again and again, until it was gone. The greatest form of surrender we'll ever know.

#LIGHTTALK

When we find our reality impacted by tragedy—whether it be the loss of a loved one, an affair, the end of a relationship, or even a diagnosis—our instinctual reflex is to go in search of answers. We look to the heavens and ask, "Why?" Because we think surely there must be a reason. Perhaps we are being punished or paying some karmic debt. Maybe it was the lie we told in grade school or the classes we skipped. Was infidelity the price I had to pay for that cigarette I smoked while out with friends when I was 17? (Marlboro menthol; one smoke and that was it for me!)

The reality is that we question because we believe the fundamental lie that we are lacking or less than. *A Course In Miracles* explains that we make the temple beautiful and adorn it when we are too afraid to approach the altar. In this metaphor, the temple is our external world and bodies, the altar is our light and truth. Why do we fear the sacredness that lies within? Perhaps because we fear it isn't there, that we are somehow deficient of light. Perhaps we suspect we were absent the day divine sparks were being implanted, because we don't remember receiving one. But that is impossible. We are all made of the same matter, our souls are woven from the same fabric, and our spark is part of a shared consciousness that connects us. It is within us all.

The course also teaches that "only love is real, nothing real can be threatened, and nothing unreal exists." In those moments of anguish and soul-crushing pain, the darkness feels very real and it can be difficult to follow spiritual principles and see our thoughts and our perceptions of our experiences not as "facts" but as illusions tinted by the lenses we choose to wear and see through—lenses of love, joy, anger, hatred, or even scarcity. Based on our perceptions of the world around us, we create a story and narrative that we project forward and choose to live in. And so with any traumatic event, experience, or tragedy, we must allow for a period to grieve what once was and no longer is. We might grieve the loss of a previous identity, an illusion of what our relationship was or could have been, the health or life we feel robbed of, and the spaces in our lives that are suddenly vacant. Instead of searching for answers or a quick path to healing, we are better served by first giving ourselves time to move through the experience and pain, allowing tears to come as often as they need to without holding them back or making people believe we are fine.

If we find ourselves uttering words like, "I just need to know why," or "I just want to understand," we are deluding ourselves into thinking these answers will provide any form of comfort. They won't. Instead we need to surrender. Surrender to the pain and the sorrow we feel, so that eventually it can be offered up to the light.

LOOKING

BEYOND

OUR OWN

PAIN AND

TO THAT

OF OTHERS

AWAKENS

COMPASSION.

CHAPTER 3

AWAKENING COMPASSION

> WE HUMANS DO NOT UNDERSTAND COMPASSION. IN EACH MOMENT OF OUR LIVES, WE BETRAY IT. AYE, WE KNOW OF ITS WORTH, YET IN KNOWING WE THEN ATTACH TO IT A VALUE, WE GUARD THE GIVING OF IT, BELIEVING IT MUST BE EARNED[...] COMPASSION IS PRICELESS IN THE TRUEST SENSE OF THE WORD. IT MUST BE GIVEN FREELY. IN ABUNDANCE.
>
> —STEVEN ERIKSON, *MEMORIES OF ICE*

EASY BUTTONS

For three years, we lived the same pattern over and over again. Every few months I would discover that communications had been reignited with the man in Mexico and our relationship would implode. I would beg and plead for my husband to put an end to the affair because of the amount of pain it was causing me. And he would, at least for a little while. Then they would begin messaging again, and we would end up right back where we started. Nothing changed—except the intensity of the rage within me.

Our fighting culminated in us spending weekends apart every few months. I would stay in the house and he would leave to spend the weekend at his friend's condo in the city. Or at least that's what I was told. In reality, those weekends were spent hopping on planes and flying out of the country to be with the man with the flowers. A fact I would eventually uncover through passport stamps and pictures on social media of weddings and events they attended together. Somehow, I had become the third wheel in my own marriage. Every time I'd ask him to break ties, he would ask for more time so that he could do it slowly so as not to hurt the man with the flowers. His lover outranked me on the scale of importance in his life. It had become clear that I needed to put my healing and well-being first; no one else was going to.

I turned to the books on my shelf and scoured the internet for a fresh approach. One evening, I came across an interview with Glennon Doyle in which she talked about her struggles with addiction. She discussed how she had turned to addiction as a form of escape from the world and to numb herself. It had become her "easy button," something she could press to avoid pain. In that moment something clicked. Perhaps my husband's infidelity was less about me and more about him. Maybe I hadn't brought this all on myself, and the repeated betrayals of my trust were a consequence of his pain and struggle. It finally occurred to me that turning to external sources of pleasure and attention outside our marriage was his easy button.

To be honest, I knew nothing about addiction, but I recognized that it had surfaced in my marriage. I saw it in his actions, and I saw it in myself. I began to recognize my own addictive patterns in how I had tried to numb the pain, first with food and later with exercise; they were my easy buttons.

While this realization didn't heal the pain I had been enduring, it did create a crack in the walls I had built around me and around my heart. I had barricaded my heart, reinforcing the walls after every betrayal, trying to keep the most precious thing I had safe. But now there was an opening, and compassion crept in. With that awakening, I was able to surrender a small part of the weight I had been carrying.

THERAPY & COMPROMISE

This awakening of compassion began to spark a cycle of healing within me, but it had done nothing to heal the broken parts of my marriage. My husband was as secretive as ever, which only further eroded my trust in him and our relationship. Everything was held under lock and key, from his cell phone to his laptop, to the drawers of his desk. And they were all password protected.

I did my best to communicate what I needed to rebuild trust and repair what had been broken. If he no longer had anything to hide, we needed to be open books. This was the only way I would ever begin to reestablish trust. My trust had been shattered so many times that the thought of it being mendable seemed almost impossible to me. But I was willing to try.

So I gave him an ultimatum: either we entered into therapy together, or I was done. Was I truly ready to walk? Probably not, but I didn't have very many cards left to play. He said he needed time to think about it, so I gave him 24 hours. The next day he agreed to counseling and, within a few hours, I had our first session booked.

Therapy was painful. We danced around the topic of infidelity without ever discussing anything outright or tackling the issue head-on. Instead, we worked on communication skills and aligning our visions for the future. But the immediate issues hadn't been resolved; in fact, they weren't even being discussed. I became a ticking time bomb. There was no atonement for anything that had transpired, nothing to rebuild my trust or bring us closer together. Instead, I felt like we were polishing the image and making everything look pretty again. My heart was reluctant to get close to him once more as, under the surface, I didn't feel like anything had changed.

One session, sitting on the opposite end of a black fake leather loveseat, with as much space between us as I could physically put, I confronted the elephant in the room. After so many betrayals of my trust and instances of infidelity, how could he possibly expect to regain my trust with everything under lock and key? Why was there a need to keep everything under password protection? He explained that his devices were personal, and he felt that giving me access would be an invasion of his privacy. My husband of seven years didn't feel comfortable with me having access to his devices. Our therapist went down the route of compromise. The two of them began a discussion about which devices he felt comfortable giving me access to and which ones he wanted to remain private. I silently watched the back and forth exchange between them like a ping pong match. Maybe the tablet could be unlocked and his phone remained private?

Finally, I exploded, yelling out in frustration, "I don't fucking care about compromise!" The two of them looked at me in shock, partially because this was the first time I had truly asserted myself, and partially because I had cursed, which is something I'm adverse to. I controlled and lowered my voice, trying my best to hide the cracks in it. Asserting myself and giving myself permission to speak up had always been extremely uncomfortable for me, and my voice shook and wavered—as it often does when we step out of our comfort zone. I explained that it was my trust that had been violated. If this was truly something he was committed to regaining and rebuilding, there was a price to be paid. I would not accept a compromise of any kind. It was access to everything, or I walked. The therapist did his best to hide the stunned look upon his face.

After much deliberation, my husband agreed to remove the passwords from his devices, an effort to wave a white flag and start the long process of rebuilding.

For the first time in a long time, I had hope. I didn't need to look through his phone or laptop; just knowing I had free access to them was enough. At least at first.

Eventually, my ego got the better of me—or, looking back, perhaps it was my intuition. My heart wanted proof that all was well so I could start to take down the barriers I had put around it. I had been misled. The passwords hadn't been removed, and the only time I had access to the devices were when we were both home together so that my use could be supervised. Every morning and every night, the passwords were changed so that my access could be controlled.

This state of affairs continued until one morning when I spontaneously decided to work from home and there wasn't time to change the passwords. The laptop was left vulnerable to my wandering eyes. That's when I found them: the chains of text messages with random men, the pictures that had been exchanged, the explicit videos that they had made together.

You used to discover an affair through lipstick on a collar, the scent of another person's perfume, or a crumpled receipt in a jacket pocket. Those were the good old days when you had to imagine the sordid scenes and images these telltale items portended. Now, in the age of technology, affairs unfolded before your eyes in a matter of seconds, showing you every explicit detail. Death by a thousand cuts.

THE RUMBLING

I came to realize that the man with the flowers was really just the tip of the iceberg. There had been so much going on beneath the surface, beyond my field of vision or awareness. My body trembled from the trauma while my lungs gasped for air. I was heartbroken.

There were no tears. I had already cried them. Instead, I looked at my life in horror, trying to understand how someone could cause so much pain. I thought back to Glennon Doyle's analogy of easy buttons and realized that only someone in immense pain could inflict this much pain onto another. That truth gave me some comfort and awakened some of the compassion that lay dormant within me, where once so much anger lay. I wondered what it must have been like for my husband to have had to hide his homosexuality for the majority of his adult life. How we fracture our souls when we go through life hiding and denying parts of ourselves in order to feel loved and accepted. Despite having come out at the age of 16, I knew what it was like to feel that there were parts of myself that weren't socially acceptable and the pain that caused. I could see how his past heartbreaks and internal struggle had left him in so much pain that he reached for outside sources of stimulation and dopamine to numb him, like a junkie looking for their next hit, but I still had to deal with the consequences of those decisions.

I wrestled with my emotions for a long time and ultimately sought further therapy and support. But what brought me the greatest sense of relief were my own practices and devotions, tending to my wounds and spending my evenings in my basement practicing kundalini meditations. They awakened me to the realization of just how much compassion I had been lacking. Not only compassion for my husband and his struggles and whatever pain pushed him to commit such hurtful acts, but compassion for myself, which manifested in my lack of assertion, the un-held boundaries, and how little respect I demanded from myself and others. My compassion had been deficient, and I had denied myself it most of all. My instinct had always been to give and provide comfort and compassion to others, first and foremost. To heal, I would have to extend the same love and empathy to myself.

#LIGHTTALK

There is no justification that can excuse poor behavior or another person offloading their pain on others, but the willingness to look beyond our own pain and to that of others begins the process of awakening compassion.

It can be extremely difficult to hold compassion for someone who may have hurt you or done you wrong. It may be a struggle to even conceive of that possibility. But the process of holding compassion for others and ourselves is where our healing journey begins. If you need help starting this process, I offer the following meditation practice.

COMPASSION MEDITATION

> Sit quietly on the floor with your legs crossed, or in a chair with your back straight and your feet planted firmly on the floor.
>
> Close your eyes and begin to breathe deeply in through your nose and out through your nose.
>
> Breathe in and breathe out.

Call into your mind's eye the image of someone you love and hold dear. Feel the warmth of your love for them surround them. Envision a blanket of light draping itself over their shoulders, shrouding them in warmth. Take time to notice its color, texture, and scent. How does compassion feel to you?

Once you can hold that image and that feeling in your heart, shift your focus to someone who may have hurt you. Someone you are struggling to have compassion for.

See their innocence at the center of their being. See the child within them that is calling out for love. If this feels uncomfortable for you, you can hold them at a greater distance or you can stop here and revisit this step next time. Everyday practice will help you get a little further in this meditation each time.

Now drape the same blanket of light over their shoulders. See it surround them. Feel them surrounded by the same love and warmth you experienced earlier.

With every inhale and exhale, see the light that surrounds them grow brighter.

If you feel called to, pray for their healing.

When you feel satisfied, slowly reconnect with your physical body, wiggling your fingers and toes.

Take a deep breath in, and exhale. And, when you feel ready, open your eyes to the room.

YOU WILL
NEVER KNOW
ACCEPTANCE
UNTIL YOU

HAVE MET

AND SAT

WITH YOUR

RESISTANCE.

CHAPTER 4

RADICAL ACCEPTANCE

> THERE ARE TWO BASIC MOTIVATING FORCES: FEAR AND LOVE. WHEN WE ARE AFRAID, WE PULL BACK FROM LIFE. WHEN WE ARE IN LOVE, WE OPEN TO ALL THAT LIFE HAS TO OFFER WITH PASSION, EXCITEMENT, AND ACCEPTANCE. WE NEED TO LEARN TO LOVE OURSELVES FIRST, IN ALL OUR GLORY AND OUR IMPERFECTIONS. IF WE CANNOT LOVE OURSELVES, WE CANNOT FULLY OPEN TO OUR ABILITY TO LOVE OTHERS OR OUR POTENTIAL TO CREATE. EVOLUTION AND ALL HOPES FOR A BETTER WORLD REST IN THE FEARLESSNESS AND OPEN-HEARTED VISION OF PEOPLE WHO EMBRACE LIFE.
>
> —JOHN LENNON

THE SHIELD OF PERFECTIONISM

Months passed, and I stopped asking questions I didn't want the answers to. I had resumed my routine of making everything look perfect on the outside; truthfully, I don't think I had ever stopped. My husband spun a tale about the videos I had found, explaining that they were old. I knew it was a lie—he was wearing his wedding ring and a new watch in them—but I swept it under the rug, for no other reason than to give myself a moment of relief. He promised he had changed, and I could see he was making a concerted effort. Reluctantly, I gave him another chance. I still held a strand of hope that my marriage could be saved.

Then, in the spring of 2015, on Easter morning, I received an unexpected call. I would need to leave the country and travel to South Africa on business for three weeks. I instantly felt a tightening in my chest. Previous indiscretions had taken place while I was away on business; given we had ended couples counseling only a few months prior, I feared the past was destined to repeat itself. It didn't seem like enough time had passed for this kind of test.

Reluctantly, I left. Off to a new adventure, halfway around the world. It was the furthest I had ever traveled but, instead of feeling excited, I was barely holding myself together. To accompany me on my flight, I brought Eckhart Tolle's book *A New Earth*. I had found it while rummaging through our household library. "Who has a home library?" you may be wondering. Someone who is trying desperately to paint the illusion of a perfect life. I had found Eckhart's book tucked away on a shelf of used books that had been given to us from a friend. It had been sandwiched between gay romances and fantasies, but something about it stood out. I pulled it off the shelf and slid it into my backpack.

I read it as continents and ocean passed far below. It provided my first exposure to the idea of the ego. In all honesty, I didn't quite get it right away and ended up revisiting passages several times. But it sparked my curiosity and gestured to the idea that perhaps there could be something more for me and for my life.

I had been going through a tough time, not just at home but at work due to recent disagreements with coworkers. My sense of self-worth had already been shattered over the previous years and months, and now, suddenly, I was questioning even my ability to do my job, the one thing I had always been certain of.

That night I had dinner with colleagues. I was about to order a cheese-less pizza in an Italian restaurant when my cell phone rang. It was my husband. In a teary voice, he told me our dog, the oldest of two, had just passed away. My heart sank and my eyes began to well up. Suddenly I couldn't manage the lie I had been living, trying to appear strong and unfazed by the outside world when inside I was devastated.

I retreated to my room, where, after a few painful Skype calls, I wept myself to sleep.

The next morning, I was too weak to move. Thankfully it was Saturday and there was nowhere I needed to be. The pain of this loss felt debilitating and, being so far from home, there was nothing I could do. Part of me felt like I had lost a child. Of course, I do not mean to compare my grief to that of someone who has actually lost a child. But for me, our dogs had taken the place of children in my life when I had abandoned all hope of starting a family, knowing that I couldn't bring a child into such a dysfunctional environment.

I spent all day under the covers, unable to eat or leave my hotel room. The hours passed and, as I lay there, I felt the pillars that held up my life crumble. I felt lost. My entire life, I had worked so hard to make everything look perfect: the house, the family, the food, the job, everything I touched. I believed the more I perfected my life, the safer I was. Safe from criticism, from judgment, from attack and shame. Now, this illusion caved in on me. Nothing was safe. Nothing was stable. I couldn't move under the weight of the rubble.

And then, from across the room, I heard an email come in on my laptop. I hadn't eaten or left the bed in hours, but something called me to go check. I stared at the screen. It was an email from Oprah. Not Oprah herself, naturally, but from her website. I had previously registered for a meditation challenge with Oprah and Deepak Chopra and must have ended up on their mailing list. The email was about a new program they were offering called "The Gifts of Imperfection," with Brené Brown, based on her book of the same title.

I had never heard of the book or of Brown; this would be my first exposure to the woman whose work would profoundly change my life. As I sat there watching the trailer for the course, I couldn't help but feel like this was exactly what I needed. I signed up instantly. That afternoon, I showered and jumped on a train to a mall in a nearby city. I had seen a bookstore there on one of my previous visits and hoped it might have a copy of the book. Sadly, it was sold out.

And so, upon my return to my hotel room, I ordered a copy on Amazon, to be delivered in time for my arrival home in Canada. But what was I to do in the meantime? I was determined not to start the online program until I was home, with both the book and a blank journal in hand. So instead, I sat, and I felt. I felt all of it. The pain, the sadness, the disappointment, mostly the shame. I had tried so hard to create the perfect life and had failed. I later learned through Brené's work that perfectionism is like a heavy shield we carry around. We think it keeps us safe but, instead, it imprisons us behind it.

ACCEPTANCE & PERMISSION

I arrived home from my trip and tried hard to settle back into my life. But there was no denying life at home had changed. We were one family member short and everyone was feeling it—including our other dog, Fiji, who had suddenly lost her sister.

Fiji had come into our lives in 2009, somewhat unplanned. She had been abandoned and was being cared for by close friends while they searched for a home for her. The minute I laid eyes on her, my heart melted. She joined our family. It was a dysfunctional family, but a family nonetheless. She had always been filled with so much love and joy and had seen me through some of the hardest moments of life over the previous years. But now, here she was, so depressed she wouldn't even leave the couch to eat. My heart ached even more.

I did the only thing I could think of. I convinced my husband that we should get another dog so she wouldn't be alone. Much like someone trying to use the idea of a baby to save their relationship, I insisted until my husband reluctantly gave in. We adopted another rescue, a five-month-old puppy named Lana. Lana means "wool" in Spanish. I felt it was a sign that she was destined for us and that everything would be ok. I had started knitting during the summer of 2009, right before I had adopted Fiji. I had been transitioning between jobs and just learned that, while no indiscretions had transpired yet, my husband was active on dating sites and chatting with other men. That was when a longtime friend, whom I affectionately call my big sister, taught me how to knit. I was immediately captivated with the ability to create something out of just some yarn and a couple of needles. Knitted pieces were fragile and yet they held together. I loved that at any moment you could slide the stiches off the needles and pull the rows apart without compromising the integrity of the yarn. My marriage and life at the time felt like a tapestry: a few stiches had been dropped along the way, but it was still holding together. I wondered, if things were to unravel, whether I could bounce back and create something new. My passion for knitting followed me through the years, and the shelves of my office were lined with balls of wool, stacked and sorted by color, moving from dark to light. During difficult moments, I would reach for a set of knitting needles. Now I hoped Lana would instill the same kind of comfort and calm in our lives. And she did.

For a while, everything was better. We felt like a family again. Lana brought new life into our home and quickly developed a bond so strong with her new sister that they couldn't be separated. The drama and pain seemed like a thing of the past and, for the first time in a long time, I felt like I could catch my breath.

With things seemingly on the mend, I dove into Brené Brown's book. I opened up a brand-new journal, dug out a set of watercolors from my office drawers, and went to work filling the pages with old pictures and letters to myself.

I started by giving myself permission. Permission to be seen, to be happy, to be wrong, to fail, even to start saying no. I wasn't sure which was harder: allowing myself to possibly fail and be wrong, or to possibly be happy. I had denied myself both for so long. In previous coaching sessions with my soul sister, I had envisioned the life I truly and deeply wanted but always saw it in the distance, sailing farther and farther away.

I continued to work with my health coach. She lived in Nevada, but we spoke every two weeks over Skype. I had initially enlisted her help to lose weight and get fit. But now she recommended I start doing things for myself, to nurture myself, when I wasn't working out. Previously my motivation had all been outwardly-focused—having convinced myself that if I got fit, and had abs, I could save my relationship. But now I began to tap into something new: self-care, or self-love, call it what you will.

To that end, prior to my trip to South Africa, I had tried my first meditation challenge—the one that had placed me on Oprah's mailing list. Which I had failed miserably at. I never got past day five of the 21-day challenge. I did repeat meditations that resonated with me every couple days or so, but I didn't really get meditation. With the amount of pain and discomfort in my life, I was extremely resistant to the idea of sitting still with nowhere to go and nothing to do but feel and be present.

I opted for something different that had similar benefits to meditation, but offered more movement and rhythm to occupy my mind. I grabbed the yoga mat I had stashed away at the back of my closet and hit the gym. The gym had become my happy place, or at least a safe place, so I was willing to explore different modalities for caring for myself within its borders.

I was still so far from the goals I had set for myself—and that vision of the future I had shared with Lara—but I began to look at myself and ask some important questions. What if I was ok? What if my body was truly fine the way it was? How differently would my life look if I began to accept myself as opposed to spending every waking hour resisting?

#LIGHTTALK

UNDERSTANDING IS THE FIRST STEP TO ACCEPTANCE, AND ONLY WITH ACCEPTANCE CAN THERE BE RECOVERY.
—J.K. ROWLING, *HARRY POTTER AND THE GOBLET OF FIRE*

The journey to radical acceptance isn't always an easy one. Mostly this is because we have developed so much resistance to who we are, based on who we think we should be and who the world tells us we should be.

Do you remember who you were before you started to take on the roles and personas that society dictated? Maybe it wasn't society. Maybe it came from within your family. We're constantly bombarded with ideals of who we need to be. We take these on because we believe these will in effect cause us to be worthy. Worthy of love, of belonging, of connection. Worthy of taking up space.

I often asked myself over the years how much of my desire to change my body was related to a longing to feel worthy of love and of being desired, and how much was simply about making myself smaller. Taking up less space in the world, in my life, and in my relationships. Being less noticeable, more inconspicuous. Being overweight, even if it was only a couple of pounds, made me feel like the elephant in the room. There was nowhere to hide. Nowhere safe or out of sight. Nowhere where the judgment or criticism of others couldn't find me.

You will never know acceptance until you have met and sat with your resistance.

If you are struggling with acceptance in your life, know that it will never come until you have faced your resistance. We must witness our resistance without judging ourselves, or judging our resistance. Instead, get curious about your resistance and engage with it.

Our resistance—like our ego, of which it is born—is designed to keep us safe. We judge and criticize ourselves and others in order to protect ourselves. By judging ourselves, we hope to lessen the blow when we receive judgment from others. We then judge others when we find the judgments of ourselves unbearable. We offload on others, in order to provide ourselves some relief.

I judged myself relentlessly. One source of my resistance lay in the erroneous belief that my worth was attached to, even dependent upon, my physical appearance and my weight. Perhaps you find yourself in the same situation or perhaps your resistance lies somewhere else. Have you ever gotten curious? Try asking yourself what your resistance is trying to protect you from.

In chapter 2 we spoke about how the ego collects evidence—evidence to support the stories we make up about ourselves, about our unworthiness and unlovability—to further its hold on us. Instead of listening to your ego, try listening to your heart. What evidence does your heart need? If we go seeking evidence of our light, we will find it. Our heart will always bring us back to the light.

The following quote is from *A Wrinkle in Time* and has guided me on my journey through acceptance and continues to do so.

DO YOU REALIZE HOW MANY EVENTS, CHOICES, THAT HAD TO OCCUR SINCE THE BIRTH OF THE UNIVERSE LEADING UP TO THE MAKING OF YOU? JUST EXACTLY THE WAY YOU ARE.
—MADELEINE L'ENGLE, *A WRINKLE IN TIME*

Our lives are part of a larger design. Each moment, each situation, conspires in its own way not against you, but for you. Our bodies are no different. We needn't remind our heart to beat or our lungs to breathe. Our bodies will metabolize thousands of meals over the course of our lives. Our legs and feet will carry us on unexpected journeys and great adventures.

We can't force or beat our lives, our bodies, or our relationships into submission. The act of constantly pushing is exhausting and highly depleting. When we surrender our resistance and make room for acceptance, we can be pulled forward, led with grace and compassion both for ourselves and others. Change begins with accepting what is and holding reverence and gratitude for what was.

Our resistance lies in our fear of change. Even positive change can provoke fear. Getting a glimpse of the potential for beauty and love that lives within you can feel unsafe. During moments of resistance, I turn to the following prayer to surrender my resistance and judgments, and instead make room for acceptance and joy.

A PRAYER FOR SURRENDER

Dear God,

I surrender to you my doubts and fears.
My thoughts of self-attack, self-judgment, and self-doubt.
I surrender these thoughts and emotions to you,
As I know that they are born of fear and not of truth.
I ask that they be transformed and transmuted,
So that I may return to a place of peace and love within myself.

I place this (situation/relationship) in your hands,
And pray for a solution that is of the highest good for all.
I pray that I be guided and shown the next right action,
So that I may live a life congruent with my purpose
To be a vessel of light and love in this world.

Amen.

AWAKENING THE **LIGHT WARRIOR** WITHIN

STORIES

CARRY

WITHIN

THEM

SOMETHING
SACRED.
SHARE THEM
WISELY.

CHAPTER 5

COURAGE AND HEART WORDS

> WHEN WE LEAST EXPECT IT, LIFE SETS US A CHALLENGE TO TEST OUR COURAGE AND WILLINGNESS TO CHANGE; AT SUCH A MOMENT, THERE IS NO POINT IN PRETENDING THAT NOTHING HAS HAPPENED OR IN SAYING THAT WE ARE NOT YET READY. THE CHALLENGE WILL NOT WAIT. LIFE DOES NOT LOOK BACK. A WEEK IS MORE THAN ENOUGH TIME FOR US TO DECIDE WHETHER OR NOT TO ACCEPT OUR DESTINY.
> —PAULO COELHO, *THE DEVIL AND MISS PRYM*

ABANDONING YOURSELF TO KEEP SOMEONE ELSE

In January of 2016, I finally found my point of no return.

A few months before the holiday season, I had found myself in the possession of a video explicitly showing me that my husband had once again been unfaithful. I was ready to walk away; for the first time ever, I was really ready. I requested that our holiday plans be canceled and our guests notified. I had no intention of receiving house guests for weeks on end as we dismantled our life together. But he begged and pleaded, insisting that the video I had found was old (it wasn't) and that things would be different now. Somehow, I still retained a thread of hope that this might be true, so I conceded and carried on with our holiday plans. We spent the days between Christmas and New Year's at a cottage in the country with his parents, my in-laws. While there, text messages came in on my husband's tablet, accompanied by explicit videos and pictures. Locked in the bedroom of the shared cabin we had rented, I felt my insides start to shake. These weren't random messages from a stranger; clearly, communication had been previously established. But they weren't from the man with the flowers, or the man in the video I had found a few months prior, or any of the other indiscretions of which I was aware. The fact they indicated a new affair was no longer unsettling; instead, it induced a sense of deep sadness within me. I felt deeply ashamed that I had once again fallen for the same lies and deceptions. Over the following days, I assumed the identity of my husband and messaged this new intruder in my marriage, trying to uncover just how far back the connection went. As if it really mattered at this point. But fueling my anger and obsession into detective work was all that was keeping me from self-destructing.

One January evening, I attended a yoga class in which I found my mind completely disconnected from my body. I have a very limited memory of the class itself; I'm not sure what poses we did, or if I even moved at all. But the movement that took place within me is still vivid. At the time, we were one month away from celebrating our 10-year anniversary and, as the class around me breathed and stretched, I looked back on the past decade, not in horror but in disbelief.

Maya Angelou once said:

WHEN SOMEONE SHOWS YOU WHO THEY ARE, BELIEVE THEM THE FIRST TIME.

My husband had shown me who he was, and the true nature of my marriage, several times, but I had chosen not to believe it.

Instead I had abandoned myself, my hopes and dreams, my needs, and more importantly my values, to keep him. That night, on my yoga mat, free from tears, I decided I was done. I had abandoned myself long enough. My husband wasn't the only one who had betrayed me; I had betrayed myself.

Best-selling author Caroline Myss says there is a distinction to be made between compromise and betrayal. A compromise that does not rob us of our values or beliefs, one that is made willingly, is truly a compromise. A compromise that causes us to violate our beliefs, our values, and in the process our soul, is a betrayal of ourselves. I firmly believe that this is the worst type of betrayal, because one of its consequences is it creates a foundation for how others can treat us.

THE COURAGE TO STAND ALONE

> **LETTING GO DOESN'T MEAN THAT YOU DON'T CARE ABOUT SOMEONE ANYMORE. IT'S JUST REALIZING THAT THE ONLY PERSON YOU REALLY HAVE CONTROL OVER IS YOURSELF.**
> —DEBORAH REBER, *CHICKEN SOUP FOR THE TEENAGE SOUL*

The next morning, I went about my day as usual, but my

mind seemed clearer, my burden lighter. Nothing was official yet, I hadn't even spoken with my husband, but my decision had been made. For the first time, I felt like I had the capacity to walk away. It had become abundantly clear that my happiness was my responsibility and mine alone. I could choose to stay in this marriage and continue living the way I had been, or I could leave. The unknown was still terrifying. There was no way to know what would await me in the future and if I'd even be happy again. Would I ever find love again? Would I ever trust again? Who would I become? What would my life look like? I had answers to none of these questions, but one thing I knew for certain. I knew exactly what my life would be like if nothing changed.

LET YOUR FEAR OF STAYING BECOME BIGGER THAN YOUR FEAR OF LEAVING.

That night we decided to part ways and let each other go. We were both exhausted from holding onto the idea of who we could be together and what our relationship could look like. Tears flowed, but neither of us tried to convince the other to stay. We had been down that road before and we knew exactly where it led. Instead, we thanked each other for everything we had learned from one another. For all the good memories. There were some, after all.

I knew that I would rather be alone and single and have a chance at happiness. My happiness, my piece of mind, were worth more than the life I had built. I deserved to be free of the knots that formed in my stomach every time my husband reached for his phone. To be free of the anxiety that accompanied every return home from a business trip, unsure of what awaited me. To be free of the panic that paralyzed me every time my husband went out with friends, wondering where the night would lead and if he'd return home.

My decision had been made, but I wasn't ready to tell anyone yet. One, because I couldn't deal with the influx of questions that I knew would follow. But also because I was still working on processing it all myself. In her book *The Gifts of Imperfection*, Brené Brown says, "Courage is a heart word." In other words, courage means to speak from one's heart. She also notes, "Our stories are not meant for everyone. Hearing them is a privilege, and we should always ask ourselves this before we share: 'Who has earned the right to hear my story?'" The truth was, except for a select few, no one had earned the right to my story. Not yet, at least.

A PLACE CALLED HOME

In the days that followed, I found myself breaking down into tears over the smallest things. Washing the dishes as I looked out the window at the yard would open floodgates. As would lying in the guestroom bed with my dogs by my side. I didn't understand it at first. I had already cried enough tears over years of heartbreak. Yet it seemed there was still more that needed to come out.

I proceeded to meet with banks and financial consultants, and spent the hours that weren't filled with work crunching numbers, trying to figure out a path forward. My biggest concern was how I could keep my home, the place into which I had poured so much love and so much of myself. From the gardens I had planted in the yard to the fireplaces I had installed, to the walls I had painted. I quickly realized that the tears I was shedding weren't for my marriage anymore; they were for my home and the very real possibility that I would lose it.

Relentlessly I tried to make the numbers add up. I would

have to take out a loan to cut my husband a substantial check to buy out his half. This meant I'd be living hand to mouth for a few years in order to survive, if I even could. To make accounts balance, I would have to get rid of a lot of luxuries, like Internet and cable. Gradually, my tears turned to rage as I realized that, to keep the house, I would have to go into debt so severely I may never recover. Meanwhile, with the check I gave him, my husband could start a new life, free from the burdens that I would now be stuck with. It seemed so unfair. After being the devoted husband for so many years, remaining faithful and loyal, these would be the cards I would be dealt. Didn't I deserve the same fresh start, the same chance at a new life, a better life? I certainly wanted it but, for it to be even remotely possible, it looked like I would have to give up even more than I had bargained for.

YOUR NEW LIFE WILL COST YOU YOUR OLD ONE.

I had clung to the idea of keeping my house because it was the only thing I had left from my 30 years on this planet. Everything else had been dismantled, or so it seemed. But I quickly realized I would have to let my old life die; that would be the price of a new one. And that meant giving up the last remains of that life that I still had: my home. I gave myself permission to mourn this final injury. And I realized I could accept it. I was giving up a house: walls, plaster, some paint, but nothing more. They didn't create the entity that I had come to know as "home." That lived within me and within the hearts of those I love. Those whom I chose to welcome into my home and life. Home was less a place and more a feeling. It was built through memories, shared laughter, and moments of peaceful silence. In that moment, I realized any place I chose would be home. As long my dogs were with me, as long as there was love and light in my heart, home could be anywhere. So, the "for sale" sign went up and I prepared myself for another unknown in the journey before me.

#LIGHTTALK

My whole life, I had made it my mission to make myself invisible when things got tough. It had been a coping strategy that had followed me from childhood, through years of bullying, and into adulthood. I brought it into my relationships, both platonic and romantic. I thought if I was invisible, I would be free from further hurt and the judgment of others. I could protect myself. But invisibility isn't safe, it's deadly. Because you don't only become invisible to others, you become invisible to yourself as well. You begin to walk through your life like it isn't yours, as if you're a spectator watching the story unfold, powerless to make a change.

I understand that invisibility feels safe because it gives us a back door to escape pain and fear. But when we fall into the trap of making ourselves invisible, we aren't truly living. To live bravely, or courageously, does not mean living without fear. Courage is choosing to show up despite being afraid. In those moments when the future seems unknown (which it always is), we live bravely by choosing to be present and continue marching forward. We must be willing to let go of the past, even if we aren't sure how. The "how" will come.

In my experience, when life hits hard, there can be a desire to tell our story in an effort to receive comfort, sympathy, and even validation. This isn't bad or wrong. But we must remember that our stories carry within them something sacred because how we tell our stories shows how we think of ourselves. Are we the villain? If our stories are self-deprecating, we certainly might be. Or are we the victim? Sometimes we all face circumstances that are outside our control: a divorce, infidelity, diagnosis, pick your poison. The problem is when we victimize ourselves through our stories, we remain trapped within them. The more we tell our stories from this perspective, the further we cement ourselves within this narrative. This can also happen when we share our stories too broadly and too quickly without processing and moving our way through them first. It is important to share our stories because our stories are usually riddled with shame, and shame needs to be spoken to be dissolved. Bury shame and it reproduces like weeds. But when we share our stories prematurely, we remove or suppress the shame-inducing elements for fear of judgment, and so our sharing is of service to no one, least of all ourselves.

Brené Brown says to tell your story to those who have earned the right to hear it. Who has earned the right to hear your story? Who holds your trust? Whose opinion truly matters? Who can you tell anything to without fear of judgment? These are our heart people, our soul brothers and sisters, and you will probably only have a few. If you can come up with a list half a page long, you're probably not being honest with yourself and are adding names to the list because you think they should be there. Maybe your husband, your mother, your best friend, don't make the list. That's ok. Maybe your list contains just 2-3 key individuals with whom you can share anything. That's ok too. If your list is even that big, you're pretty fortunate.

These individuals have earned the right to hear our stories. They have gained our trust and been there for us, not for the big, shiny moments but for the little moments that otherwise sucked. These are the people who call to check in, or who ask what is on your mind because the light in your eyes doesn't seem as bright as usual. Secrets shared with them remain secrets. They respect that your story is yours to tell, and yours alone.

We should share our stories with these people because we can share the whole story, even the parts that bring us shame. This allows us to bring the dark parts out into the light. Sharing the ugliness of your story with someone you trust, that's courage. When you open your heart and dare to be vulnerable, that's living bravely. It won't be easy, even with the people we trust, our heart people, but this is where deep healing begins. Where we bring our wounds to the light so we can heal. To be brave in the world, we need these small, safe spaces in which we work through our fear and shame. Once we begin the process of releasing our shame, we can reach acceptance and, with it, new possibilities will begin to emerge for a life that is truly beautiful.

EXERCISE

Make a list of your heart people, whom you feel you can share freely with. Grab a pen and paper, and actually write them down. There is something healing about putting pen to paper as opposed to making a list in our heads. It stimulates different parts of our brain and anchors our actions further in our subconscious.

You should need no more than a square inch of paper to write down the names because that's how short it should be.

Validate the names on your list. Ask yourself: would you share your deepest, darkest secrets with this person without fear of being judged? It may still feel scary to share due to the vulnerability of exposing your darkness, but it shouldn't stem from fear of judgment. If the people on your list don't pass this gauge, keep searching. We often make this harder than it has to be by believing that certain names need to be on our lists: our partners, a sibling, parents, maybe our best friend. But if none of these people feel right for your list, that's perfectly fine. It doesn't mean they won't make it onto your list in the future. For now, concentrate on where you feel safe.

Most of us have one person we can share anything with, but what if you don't? Put it out to the Universe. Pray for your spiritual running buddy to find their way into your life, and trust that your prayer will be answered. Until then, you can look to online forums that are dedicated to spiritual growth; these are usually among the safest. Before you share, read through the posts and look at the comments others are receiving; this will tell you a great deal about the integrity of the group. If all else fails, grab a journal and freewrite. Set yourself aside some time, play some relaxing music in the background, and let it all flow onto the page. Don't read what you've written or stop to correct grammar or spelling. Let it flow without editing your thoughts or emotions.

What is the story that you're carrying that holds the most amount of shame? Usually, these stories are creating the narrative of our lives and the lens through which we view the world. Share it with one of your heart people, in a safe online space, or in your journal. Bringing it to the light will start to release it from your body, making room for healing.

RELEASE THE GOD YOU WERE GIVEN

TO FIND

THE

GOD YOU

NEED.

CHAPTER 6

CENTERING, GROUNDING, AND CLARITY

AT THE CENTER OF YOUR BEING YOU HAVE THE ANSWER; YOU KNOW WHO YOU ARE AND YOU KNOW WHAT YOU WANT.
—LAO TZU

TELL ME WHO I SHOULD BE

I spent most of my life struggling with who I should be. Who did the world need me to be? Who did I need to be in order to fit into this world? It was not surprising that I had brought this uncertainty into my marriage and my previous relationships. I had grown up overweight, obese by some definitions, which made my early years difficult. I'll never forget my parents taking me to a seamstress to have pants custom-made for me. I was only eight or nine years old, and fairly short, but children's clothes no longer fit me, and adult clothing, while suitable in circumference, didn't come in the right length.

I was bullied in school for the lethal combination of being fat, wearing glasses, and doing well in school. Children can be particularly hurtful in their teasing and bullying. During my childhood and teenage years, I gravitated towards people who were different, which made sense: I felt different too. Although I didn't have many friends and was never one of the popular kids, I had groups of friends, and in these groups, I fit in and felt accepted. I had spaces where I felt safe. High school was a particularly confusing time. When I started high school, I was still overweight, which made me a target for bullying. I tried to make myself invisible by remaining quiet and soft-spoken, in hopes that I could fade into the crowd and coast through. But when you stand out physically, it can be hard to stay under the radar. I became increasingly aware of my body. I wasn't athletic or good at sports; I could barely jog the track. Eating at school became one of the things I most dreaded each day. In fact, eating in public, in general, induced anxiety, for fear that people would judge what I ate and my size as a result. I would go out for lunch with friends and order only water, spinning a story of having eaten earlier or of having had a big breakfast or an upset stomach.

I was fortunate that a physical education teacher took an interest in me in my third year of high school. She saw that I just didn't excel at team sports and introduced me to weight training and track and field, activities where I wasn't forced to rely on team members and where the only competition I could cultivate was with myself. In these activities, the point was striving to get better. This was perhaps my first exposure to the idea of self-betterment, although I was too invested in ideals and stereotypes at the time, trying to figure out which box I belonged in, to fully benefit from it. Nevertheless, by running and working out, I lost weight. I still had issues around food, but socially things got better. I felt more accepted than I had been before. Then—later that same year—I realized I was gay. It was just something else to set me apart. I told a few of my closest friends, but I kept it pretty quiet for a few months to give myself some time to understand what being gay meant for me and for my life. That time ended abruptly when a rumor that I was gay spread through the school. I was faced with a choice: I could lie and deny it, knowing that doing so would only invite further teasing and bullying, or I could accept my newfound truth and be open about it. I chose the latter, becoming one of the few openly gay kids in school. I'd like to say that it was easy, but it wasn't. Two horrible years of teasing, bullying, and name-calling followed. I began to skip school, and my grades declined. I missed so many classes it was a miracle that I graduated at all.

In my final year, a few months before graduation, I took the stage during an annual assembly and spoke publicly in front of the entire school about the discrimination and bullying faced by members of the LGBT community. I began my talk by yelling the profanities and names I had been called as I walked through the school hallways, eliciting gasps throughout the auditorium. My frank approach earned me some respect among my classmates, and my last few months were surprisingly better. But it didn't change the more fundamental problem: I had no idea who I was meant to be.

I went to pride parades with friends and hung around the Village but, within the community in which I was supposed to be safe and free to express myself, I found more labels and stereotypes than I had faced from the outside looking in. I wasn't flamboyant, or extroverted, or promiscuous. I didn't identify with any of the labels and wasn't into the party scene. I ultimately alienated myself from the community and resorted to online dating to meet people and make new connections. Initially, this didn't go well; at one point, I had to deal with an actual stalker. But, eventually, I met the man who would be my future husband—and then ex-husband.

Once we met, I accelerated the timeline to create the life

I thought I was supposed to have. We dated, moved in together, and got engaged within a year, and were married the following fall. This was supposed to set us up to buy a house and eventually start a family. I settled into the role of homemaker, with Martha Stewart as my role model, and threw myself into building a life and home that would look perfect, at least on paper and to the outside world.

But it never felt quite right. There were red flags from the beginning, even in the early years of our marriage, but I turned a blind eye. This was still the shortest path to the life I thought I should want. It was only with the implosion and ultimately the end of my marriage that I began to strip back the layers of who I really was and, more importantly, what I wanted.

As my marriage disintegrated, my childhood body image issues resurfaced. In addition to my issues with weight, I worried that I wasn't handsome enough. I certainly didn't have enough hair! Mine had started thinning years earlier, a combination of hereditary genes and stress. I became resentful, plagued by the idea that I had given my most attractive years to someone who wasn't worthy of them. I was only going to get older. With age and time taking their toll, what kind of future could I possibly expect?

I began to hate the way I looked, even as I worked out relentlessly. When I looked in the mirror, I don't think I ever really saw myself. Instead, all I saw was the faults and lacks that I had projected onto myself. I hated taking pictures and yet resented the fact that my husband was always taking pictures and selfies, often with friends, some of whom were more than friends. He never seemed to want to take pictures of or with me; my presence or role in his life went unacknowledged. Probably because it would have made it harder to live a double life.

YOGA & MANTRAS

After my marriage ended, I wanted and craved a new way of being. A new way of showing up in the world. For a while, as I discussed earlier, that manifested in spending hours in the gym, working out twice per day most days. I believed that maxing out my caloric expenditure each day would get me where I wanted to go. That by losing weight and getting shredded, I would be worthy of the attention and love of others. But over time, I began to realize that this was my easy button. I was falling into the same old patterns of thought. A new way of being would require a new way of thinking.

In the months just preceding the end of my marriage, my health coach had recommended I take a few days a week off from training and try something lighter like yoga. She thought it might help reduce the strain I was putting on myself and my body. I had tried yoga a decade before on a cruise ship with an ex-boyfriend and found it incredibly dull and boring, but I was willing to give it another go. She also recommended I take up meditation (something else I had dabbled in previously) and put aside some time for myself each day. This was years before self-love and self-care became a trend. Initially I brushed off the idea of meditation, but agreed to give yoga a try, thinking it might help release some of the soreness and stiffness I had been experiencing. I grabbed my mat and returned to the same classroom where I had come to the realization that my marriage was finally over.

The challenge of yoga got me hooked. Right away I was intrigued by the possibility of someday being able to bend and twist like our yoga instructor, or possibly even do handstands. Our instructor moved and flowed into each position effortlessly and with so much grace, her body seemed weightless and light. It was the opposite of how I felt or thought about myself. I knew I wanted some of that.

I quickly learned that yoga wasn't about forcing or pushing your body, something I had always done. Instead, it required you to work with it, and gradually expand and grow its capabilities, slowly pushing the boundaries of its limitations.

DO NO HARM

"Do no harm" was one of the basic yoga sutras I learned that had a profound impact on me. It inspired me to reflect on how I could care for and love myself without inflicting pain or suffering on my own being or others. Yoga class became a healing sanctuary without my realizing. At the start of every class, I sat in Balasana (Child's Pose), connecting to my breath. And at the end of each class, I lay on the floor in Savasana (Corpse Pose) and recited a prayer to myself, a mantra I had created to nourish myself and shift my thoughts and beliefs. I lay there in the dark room, perfectly still, metabolizing the movements and practice of our class, while reciting the words to myself over and over again.

> I am loved,
> I am held,
> I am healthy,
> I am strong,
> I am flexible,
> I am attractive,
> I am handsome,
> I am worthy,
> I am enough.

LIFTING THE CRAZY FOG

Over time, I began to believe these words and see myself differently. It was as if a fog had begun to lift. I affectionately referred to it as "the crazy fog." For perhaps the first time, I began to see myself more clearly. When I looked at my reflection in the mirror every morning, I stopped cringing and focusing on my flaws or the parts of myself I told myself were ugly or not quite right. Instead I began to like what I saw. Even though nothing had physically changed—I hadn't lost weight or changed my hair—but it felt like something had changed. I began to wonder if this was always what I looked like. How long had this crazy fog been distorting my perception and to what extent?

I finally took up my health coach's second piece of advice and began to meditate daily, using meditations I found on YouTube or those referenced by the books and teachers I had been following. Without realizing it, I had begun to cultivate a spiritual practice. Mantras and meditations became the support structure that got me from one day to the next. And their effect on me radiated outward. I looked different. My eyes seemed softer, my smile brighter than it had been in a long time, my soul felt lighter.

> **THERE IS A WAY OF LIVING IN THE WORLD THAT IS NOT HERE, ALTHOUGH IT SEEMS TO BE. YOU DO NOT CHANGE APPEARANCE, THOUGH YOU SMILE MORE FREQUENTLY. YOUR FOREHEAD IS SERENE; YOUR EYES ARE QUIET.**
> —*A COURSE IN MIRACLES*

#LIGHTTALK

Beginning a spiritual practice required me to grapple with my past. I had had a difficult relationship with religion and the church growing up. God and I weren't on great terms. For a long time, I referred to this higher power as "the Universe," or "Spirit." It took years before I was comfortable using the word "God." But my studies through *A Course In Miracles* taught me that, if nothing else, semantics were in fact just that: semantics. If people from different cultures and languages could all pray and have their prayers answered, then surely the divine power transcended language and labels. Clearly God was too evolved to hold grudges if we recognized Him (or Her) by another name.

TO FIND THE GOD I NEEDED, I NEEDED TO RELEASE THE GOD I WAS GIVEN.

Growing up I had been taught that God was vengeful and spiteful, and to be feared. The church further separated me from my relationship with God. Once I identified as a gay man, I was pronounced a sinner and condemned to hell. But none of this truly resonated with me. I felt like God was surely above all that. If God had created us in His image, if we were all Children of God, then He knew what he had created. Surely our ability to love one another and do good in the world was more important than our gender and sexuality, or the strictures set down in a really old book. I came to understand the Bible as man's interpretation, the retelling of a story. Just like a game of telephone, it made sense to me that some of the messages had become distorted or misunderstood over time.

When I began to develop a new spiritual practice as an

adult, I had to start by identifying and understanding what a higher power meant to me. I had felt the presence of the divine and its guidance several times over the course of my journey. It had led me and protected me, and I probably wouldn't be here without its love and guidance. But what was it? Thinking about it one day, I recalled a memory from my childhood. I was sitting in my dad's minivan while we drove somewhere, looking up at the sun in the sky. I remember thinking, "God is like a giant diamond in the sky." We are all seeing different sides of the same diamond, and we call it by different names based on our upbringing, our culture, and even our geographical location, but we're all talking about the same thing.

I came to understand that the God I had been brought up to fear was a God that we had created in our own image. We had given Him human traits and the afflictions of fear and ego. Now I could see this was a lie. God wasn't here to punish or judge us; we certainly do a good enough job of that ourselves. God was purely, and simply, Love, the fiber that connects all of us through our shared humanity.

DEFINING YOUR HIGHER POWER & CURATING A SPIRITUAL PRACTICE

In this exercise, I want to invite you to explore what a higher power means to you. Developing this understanding will support you in creating and curating a spiritual practice as well as guide you through the remainder of this book and its practices.

Take some time to settle yourself into a quiet spot where you won't be disturbed or interrupted. Perhaps put on some soft music and light a candle or some incense—

whatever you feel will support you through this exercise. Have a journal and pen close at hand.

Close your eyes and sit quietly with your legs crossed or in Sukhasana (Easy Pose), or in a chair with your back straight and feet planted firmly on the floor.

Breathe deeply, inhaling and exhaling through your nose and allowing your breath to become rhythmic and effortless.

With your eyes closed, begin to envision a golden ball of light in the center of your mind. This is the light and love of the divine, your higher power. As you breathe, allow the light to grow brighter and brighter. The ball of light gets bigger and bigger with each exhale. Let the light grow until it completely encompasses the landscape of your mind and all you can see is light. Spend a few minutes sitting and basking in the glow of this light, letting it surround you, feeling held in its presence. Stay here in this energy for as long as you like to gather the insight or wisdom you may be receiving, or simply to bask in this light.

When you are ready, take another deep breath in, letting your mind begin to settle back into your body, wiggling your fingers and toes. When you are ready, open your eyes to the room. Grab your journal and begin to free-write answers to the following statements and questions.

When I am in alignment with my higher power, I feel...

I feel most aligned and connected with my higher power when I...

What would it feel like if I was in constant connection to my higher power?

How does it feel when I rely on and surrender to my higher power?

I feel disconnected from my higher power when I...

When things feel difficult or the path ahead seems blocked, what is my higher power trying to tell me?

How do I receive messages from my higher power? (Gut feelings/intuition, hearing, sight/images, smells/physical sensations, etc.)

WHAT WE CHOOSE TO SEE IN OTHERS,

WE WILL

ALSO SEE

WITHIN

OURSELVES.

CHAPTER 7

FORGIVENESS: FOR YOU, NOT THEM

FORGIVING IS NOT FORGETTING; IT'S ACTUALLY REMEMBERING—REMEMBERING AND NOT USING YOUR RIGHT TO HIT BACK. IT'S A SECOND CHANCE FOR A NEW BEGINNING. AND THE REMEMBERING PART IS PARTICULARLY IMPORTANT. ESPECIALLY IF YOU DON'T WANT TO REPEAT WHAT HAPPENED.
—DESMOND TUTU

FORGIVENESS & BOUNDARIES

It was the early months of 2016. My husband and I had recently decided to separate, the house was on the market waiting for a buyer, and I was in unchartered waters. We were still living under the same roof as we waited for our home to sell and carpooling to work every day because I was the only one with a driver's license. Besides work and the gym, I had very few moments of refuge when I wasn't forced to confront the reality of my situation. Watching my life fall apart and everything change made me furious. And while I got more and more mad, my husband seemed more carefree and liberated than ever. "How unfair," I thought. I was paying the ultimate price for my loyalty, and yet carrying the heaviest burden.

It was during this time in limbo that I realized I needed to forgive. Not because my husband needed my forgiveness, but because I needed it. I need to forgive him, and I needed to forgive myself for not respecting and upholding my boundaries. On our very first date, over cups of hot chocolate, I had said that cheating was intolerable. We had both agreed on that point. Now I needed to forgive myself for staying after it transpired, the first time and every time after that. I needed to forgive myself for succumbing to my weakness and my ego's lies that I wasn't good enough and that this was what I deserved. I needed to forgive myself for not vocalizing what I needed to be the best version of myself. I needed to forgive myself for being in the wrong place and wrong relationship at the wrong time. I needed to forgive myself for staying silent and not telling anyone what I was going through because of the shame I felt.

During this time, I stumbled upon the work of Reverend Desmond Tutu and began to truly understand the inner workings of forgiveness. I wasn't forgiving to accept or condone my husband's infidelity; I was forgiving to release myself from it. The idea that it was for me, and no one else, seemed selfish in a way, which felt both wrong and exciting at the same time. I had spent so much of my life putting the needs of others before my own that doing something selfish was intoxicating. From my studies of *A Course In Miracles*, I knew that I needed to forgive in order to process my pain and truly move through it and not around it. I wanted to avoid having to relearn the same lessons in future relationships.

ANY MOMENT IN WHICH WE DO NOT CARRY THE WEIGHT OF THE PAST INTO THE PRESENT, WE ARE REBORN.

Forgiveness was about freeing myself from the burden of these experiences in an effort to release the negative and fragmented energy that didn't align with my truth. The question became; "How?" How do I forgive when I'm still so angry?

START WITH WILLINGNESS

My resistance to forgiveness stemmed not from unwillingness, but from my perception that my husband didn't deserve my forgiveness. It felt as if forgiveness would make his betrayal ok and let him off the hook. If I wasn't holding him accountable for his actions, then who would? The moment I was able to articulate that thought, I recognized the enormous burden I had placed upon myself. I wasn't responsible for his actions or for making him pay his karmic debt. It wasn't my place to hold him accountable. He had a conscience and a moral compass. He was more than capable of doing that on his own.

The question became; "How do I forgive and release us both, regardless of whether I think he is deserving?" And how do I deal with my own resistance and struggle with whether or not he deserves forgiveness? The answer came from within: start by being willing to forgive. And so I did.

WE DO NOT HEAL THE PAST BY DWELLING THERE, WE HEAL THE PAST BY LIVING FULLY IN THE PRESENT.
—MARIANNE WILLIAMSON

Not knowing how or where to begin actually became my prayer. During my daily meditation, and in other moments of stillness throughout the day, I would whisper to myself, "I am willing to forgive; show me how, tell me where to start."

Little did I know I had already started. Asking for guidance and declaring my intent were the first steps to get me started on my journey through forgiveness. I would be led the rest of the way.

THE OTHER PERSON IS YOU.
—YOGI BHAJAN

Not long after, I stumbled across this quote from Yogi Bhajan through the work of Gabrielle Bernstein; "The other person is you." My initial response was, "WTF?" How could he be me? I was loyal, kind, respectful, and patient. I had never cheated or been unfaithful. I rejected the idea at first, and then reflected on it—somewhat obsessively—for days after. Finally one afternoon in the shower—where most of my ideas hit me, including the idea for this book—I made the connection. I thought back to Glennon Doyle's description of easy buttons, and how we turn to different addictions—drugs, alcohol, technology, sex, etc.—in order to numb ourselves and relieve ourselves from pain. While I couldn't relate to being unfaithful, I could relate to the feeling of being in pain and wanting to numb myself. My weapon of choice was usually food. Which made me not so different from him. For the first time, I could see him as someone in pain who didn't know how to process it. And where there is pain, there is also an inherent goodness and innocence.

My forgiveness practice became my daily meditation, which I will outline below. Once I began to realize the release it gave me, it began to grow and include others for whom I had carried grievances: former lovers, friends, family members, acquaintances. Some of these grievances required daily repetitions; others were easier to release. I made it a ritual to sit in my bedroom with a candle lit, incense wafting through the air, and meditation music playing in the background. Of course none of these were essential to fostering forgiveness, but they allowed me to quickly settle into that frame of mind every evening and helped cultivate a practice that would serve me for years.

Every night, sitting on the edge of my bed with dogs to either side of me, I would call up images of those I was working on forgiving, and I would send them love—as much love as I could muster—until love was all I saw. Some days were harder than others. On these days, the pain was more vivid, and I kept those I sought to forgive at a distance during my meditation. Sometimes, I simply called them by name and stopped there if that was all I felt I could handle. There was no judgment of my practice, and I allowed myself to feel and do whatever felt right in that moment.

Cord cutting also became a regular practice during this time. Since there was no physical separation between my husband and me—we still lived under the same roof, commuted to work in the same car, and shared common living spaces despite sleeping in different rooms—energetic connections continued to form. These would feel immensely draining and would retrigger old wounds and pain. To lessen the impact of these connections, I used a cord-cutting practice by Gabrielle Bernstein, one of the many mentors who entered my life over this period. (I never met any of these mentors, but I was guided by them through the lessons in their books, as I hope you might be guided by this book.)

Energetic cords and connections form all the time without our awareness of them. Everyone we interact with throughout our day is connected to us, and us to them, through the fields of energy that surround us all. Cords form, to different degrees, like strings or strands of spaghetti, radiating outwards from us and attaching to the people around us: lovers, family members, parents, children, co-workers, acquaintances, the list goes on. These cords make us more intuitive and empathic towards the needs of others because we can feel and sense what is going on. This isn't necessarily a bad thing, but all cords should be cleared periodically, even the cords that attach us to those we love.

Sitting in meditation, I would begin the practice by evoking an image of the Archangel Michael, a luminous being of light, standing tall and wielding a large sword. I would pray to him to cut the energetic cords between myself and my husband so that only love remained. I would envision strings of glowing white light radiating out from me, connecting me and my husband, and Archangel Michael cutting through them with his sword. As the cords separated and fell to the ground, I would see them dissolve and the energy return to the earth so that it could be recycled and repurposed.

This practice always brought me a sense of peace. Once the cords had been cut, I would feel light, like a portion of my burden had been lifted. It didn't make me feel re-energized or invigorated. Instead, it instilled a sense of quiet stillness that allowed me to drift effortlessly into a peaceful night's sleep. Free from the worries of my day-to-day life and the shifting terrain of my relationship. I did this meditation as often as necessary, envisioning cords that not only connected me with my husband but with members of my family and those I loved as well. Even if we don't have a particular grievance with someone, there may still be cords of energy attaching and connecting us that are unintentionally draining us of our energy. This practice helped free me of the burden of those cords so I could appreciate those relationships for the love and magic they brought to my life.

Severing these cords can be particularly important to allow for space for healing so forgiveness can take place. This may be especially useful in situations where physical separation can't be granted, as in my case. In other circumstances, we may be able to physically separate ourselves from each other, erecting boundaries to allow space for healing to occur.

One last note about forgiveness that we often overlook: the act of forgiving someone does not mean that they need to continue to occupy a space in your life. It doesn't mean you have to invite them to your wedding or have regular lunches or message them every day. You don't need to buy them a gift for the holidays or reincorporate them into your life in any way. Forgiving someone simply means that you are releasing them. Instead of allowing them to take up space in your life, you are sending them love and blessings, and not harboring ill thoughts or wishes for them. It means you have let go of the past so you can start fresh in the present. Forgiving is not forgetting. If you have to set up boundaries in order to prevent yourself from reliving the same experience and pain, so be it. You are the most important person in this process. Put yourself first.

#LIGHTTALK

I believe there is good in everyone. We all have an innocence, a spark, within us. It cannot be altered or diminished, because it is not of us. Some call it "Spirit," others "God," others "the Universe." Whatever you choose to name this force, we are it, and it is us. Through it, we are all connected; we are all the same. So there is always something within us that is inherently good. We may forget that it's there or turn away from it, but we cannot alter or diminish it. Our journey through forgiveness allows us to see/remember that innocence/spark in others. And in those moments when we do, those holy and magical instants, we allow the people we forgive to see it in themselves too. We bestow grace and, in doing so, give others the opportunity to reconnect with themselves, provided they are willing.

In this way, the act of forgiveness is the most beautiful blessing we can bestow upon ourselves and others. For what we choose to see in others, we will also see within ourselves. When we look at others through the lens of judgment, we turn that same lens on ourselves. But when we choose to look at others through the lens of love and compassion, we will see traits in them we later see in ourselves.

Yogi Bhajan also said, "If you can't see God in all, you can't see God at all." Being able to see God or the inherent goodness in everyone, including those who have harmed us, is essential to the process of forgiving others and releasing ourselves. Even if they don't see it themselves, even if it is hard to see, knowing that it is there will release you from the burden you are carrying and allow you to move forward.

IF WE WOULD LISTEN TO THE STORIES OF OUR ENEMIES' SUFFERING, THEY WOULD NO LONGER BE OUR ENEMIES.

Pray for those you need to forgive. Pray for them as you would pray for yourself. Pray that they be loved, that they be happy, that they be blessed, that they experience joy and peace. Don't pray that they find the right path or are shown the light or the errors of their ways. Doing so would imply a judgment that they aren't on the right path, which we cannot know. Prayer and judgment cannot live within the same space. Our judgments stem from our fear-based mind and the notion that we are separate from one another. To judge others is to simultaneously judge ourselves and, when we do so, we block the path to forgiveness.

Take five minutes a day for 30 days and pray for those you want to forgive. At the end of those 30 days, you will find that either the relationship itself has transformed, or your reaction and relationship to that person has changed. You may find yourself no longer burdened or hurt by their actions and words. Once you reach that peaceful place, you'll understand what it truly means to be reborn in the present and start new.

FORGIVENESS MEDITATION

> Sit quietly on the floor or on a cushion with your legs in Sukhasana (Easy Pose) or Padmasana (Lotus Pose), or in a chair with your feet planted firmly on the floor and your back straight.
>
> Begin to breathe, slowly and deeply, inhaling and exhaling through your nose. Allow your breathing to become rhythmic and effortless.
>
> Begin with a prayer for the person or persons you are working on forgiving. One of these people may be yourself. Pray that they be loved, that they be healthy and free, that they be at peace, that they be happy, that they know joy.
>
> Don't get overly attached to the words. Allow whatever sentiments are coming through you to flow. Don't judge your words or thoughts; simply allow them to move through you. Intention here is more important than semantics.

Once you've completed your prayer and blessing, take a few moments and bring the image of the person you wish to forgive into the center of your mind. See them standing before you as you sit and meditate. If this feels too close for comfort, envision them further away, perhaps somewhere else in the world.

Envision a ball of golden light forming in the center of your chest, growing brighter and brighter. See it pulse like a beating heart, growing stronger and stronger.

Envision a beam of light beginning to stream out from the ball of light, to the person in front of you, landing in the center of their chest. Continue to stream light to this person; this is the light of love and compassion. Your light will not fade or diminish as a consequence, as the light of love is abundant and unending.

Let the light in the center of their chest grow stronger and begin to spread throughout their body, growing brighter and brighter. Allow the light to grow bigger and bigger until it extends beyond their physical body and you can no longer see the person before you. Their shape or silhouette will no longer be visible; all you will see is light. All that remains is love.

Stop streaming light from your heart to theirs and just sit in the presence of the light before you. Say a prayer to a higher power of your own understanding—God, Spirit, Love, the Universe, whichever speaks to you. Declare to your higher power that you are handing this person over to it, that you are placing them and your relationship with them in its hands. Declare that this burden is no longer yours to carry, and end by thanking your higher power.

Continue to breathe, slowly settling back into your body. With your eyes still closed, place your hands over your heart, at the center of your chest, and say a final thank you to your higher power for taking this from you. And, when you're ready, open your eyes.

Take a few moments to settle back into your body and the present moment and, if you feel called to, use this time to freewrite in a journal. Reflect on this experience, let your words flow onto the page, free from judgment.

Repeat this meditation daily, or as often as necessary.

TIME
DOESN'T
HEAL OR
ERASE

WOUNDS: IT JUST SHROUDS THEM.

CHAPTER 8

SELF-LOVE: NOT THE SAME AS SELF-CARE

IF YOU DON'T LOVE YOURSELF, HOW IN THE HELL YOU GONNA LOVE SOMEBODY ELSE?
— RUPAUL

DEPRESSION, MONO, & LETTING THE HEAVINESS SETTLE

By early 2017, we had finally sold the house, and I had moved into my own place. The preceding six months had been a whirlwind between moving, getting settled in my new home, and restoring relationships that I had pushed aside during my divorce. I also found myself spending a lot of time with my family due to a sudden event.

Prior to the holidays at the end of 2016, my father had fallen sick. He lost sensation in, and functionality of, both his legs. His situation continued to degrade, forcing him to use a cane to get around, and later a walker. Eventually he had no mobility left and required hospitalization. All the while, we anxiously awaited a diagnosis; the doctors had no clue as to what was going on with his body. (He was later diagnosed with Guillain-Barré Syndrome, a rare neurological disorder). Over the Christmas holidays, he remained in the hospital, but we were able to have him released for Christmas Day so that we could gather the family and break bread together.

It had been a tough year. The divorce, moving, and rushing back and forth to the hospital after my workday was taking its toll. There were still boxes piled around my home, but I pushed them aside and made room so that we could be together.

Gathering the family together had always been something I enjoyed. It was one of my "Martha" traits and gave me a lot of pleasure and fulfillment. In the last years of my marriage, I had done less of that, alienating myself from everyone. Now it filled me with joy to have my close family around the table, eating and partaking in conversation. It brought me back to simpler times. There's always been something about gathering with family and friends over a meal that felt like home. It was something I felt at my center; it was how houses became homes, turning strangers into friends and friends into family. It allows us a glimpse of what truly connects us: love.

Over the course of the winter, my father made a slow but gradual recovery, eventually regaining his mobility. It was a huge relief for us all, but I struggled to regain a sense of hope and lightness. I had emerged from the shadows of all that had transpired in 2016 slightly worse for wear. And now, as the months progressed, I fell deeper and deeper into the darkness. I could barely pull myself out of bed in the morning to get ready for work. My alarm would ring faithfully every morning at 5 a.m., and I would hit the snooze button repeatedly for 2-3 hours.

I felt more lifeless and depressed than I ever had before in my life. Even the worst moments of my marriage were nothing compared to the heaviness I felt then. I had studied nutrition and holistic health so I knew that the food I was eating wasn't the issue. It felt more like depression, although

I couldn't understand why. I had nothing to be depressed about. Life was good. My father had regained his health. I had settled into a home that I absolutely loved. I was happy at work, and had launched my own coaching business over the previous months. Why was I depressed?

I finally met with my doctor to have blood work done, convinced that something must be wrong with me or that I must be sick, only to find nothing. My results were normal, aside from some difficulty absorbing vitamins and minerals, mostly iron. I was devastated, not to find out that I wasn't sick, but to find out that we didn't know what was wrong. Sometimes the lack of a diagnosis feels worse; if you don't know what's wrong with you, how can you find a solution for it?

This went on for months. Even the simplest of chores, like vacuuming the house or washing dishes, started to feel monumental and excruciating to my body. I felt like I had been beaten; every muscle in my body was tired and ached.

For months, I searched for answers and, finally, in the fall of 2017, I received one. I had contracted Epstein-Barr virus (EBV)—often referred to as "mono" or "the make-out virus" due to the number of people who contract it in their teen years or early adulthood by kissing someone who has been infected. I didn't have any interesting stories to tell about how I had contracted it; no kissing here. Instead I discovered that EBV is also known as "the caretaker virus" because it often infects women who take on the role of tending to others and not themselves, eventually weakening their immune systems and becoming susceptible to the virus. One common side effect of EBV is a temporary reduction in the body's ability to absorb iron. Suddenly everything started to make sense. The effects of EBV—the tiredness, the aches, the difficulty getting out of bed—can last up to six months after the virus has been contracted. I had no choice but to just accept it and give my body the rest it needed.

For the first time in a long time, it felt good not to fight against my body, not to push through another workout or a late night of project work. Instead I had to just settle into my body in its current state, letting the heaviness and aches exist and run out their course. Of course, I did take some steps to help my body renew itself and regain my energy and strength—among them the daily consumption of celery juice and smoothies spiked with cilantro, following some of the work from Anthony William's *Medical Medium*. But otherwise this became a lesson and exercise in slowing down and caring for myself. I had run myself into the ground, never taking a minute to just absorb everything I had been through over the past decade, trial after trial, project after project, and well, it all caught up with me.

SELF-LOVE AS DEVOTION

They say that time heals all wounds. In my life, I've found this not to be true. Time doesn't heal or erase wounds, it just shrouds them. The way we heal wounds is by choosing to take of ourselves first. Left unattended and ignored, wounds will never heal themselves through the passing of time; instead they fester and steep until they are ready to pop up again in our lives.

Over the years I had spent a lot of time focusing on self-care. Whenever something seemed to be off, I thought the answer was always more self-care: more time to myself, more taking care of myself, more tending to my health—be it physical, mental, emotional, or spiritual. Self-care involves acts of kindness and love that we bestow upon ourselves. These acts tend to our needs. For example, curling up under a blanket in front of a movie, vowing not to check emails or social media, drawing ourselves a bubble bath, lighting a few candles, steeping a cup of tea, or settling in with a good book.

These activities and acts of self-care are vital for our well-being and for restoring our energy and focus. They allow us to unplug from the world around us and plug back into Source energy—the divine energy of the Universe that ebbs and flows all around. Self-care bring us back into alignment with this energy and strengthens our connection to our understanding of a higher power and ourselves.

Through my experience with EBV, I learned that there was something bigger than self-care: self-love. Self-care is prescriptive. It's the little things that we do to put ourselves back into alignment or to recharge our batteries. Self-love, on the other hand, is a practice. It's not prescriptive; it's medicine that can deeply heal us. Self-love reduces our need for all the little moments of self-care, because it becomes a lifestyle. A new way of being.

SELF-LOVE IS COMPOSED OF THREE ESSENTIAL TRUTHS: SELF-COMPASSION, SELF-AWARENESS, AND SELF-ACCEPTANCE.

Self-compassion, just like compassion for others, requires the removal of judgment. It means taking a step back when you find yourself being self-critical or self-judgmental and extending yourself compassion. It requires you to look beyond the criticism, beyond the fear, and really tend to your wounds. Once you've truly learned to practice self-compassion, your compassion towards others will be naturally transformed. The truth is we can't be compassionate towards others if we don't know how to be compassionate towards ourselves. I have always tried to be kind and compassionate towards others, but sometimes I found myself judging certain individuals, thinking they didn't deserve my kindness or compassion. Even though those judgments weren't present all the time, they affected my ability to empathize. When I began to practice self-compassion, those judgments melted away. I was able to see that the reason I was judging whether or not they deserved my compassion was precisely the reason why they did.

The second component of self-love is self-awareness. This is composed of awareness, knowledge, and wisdom. Self-awareness involves recognizing when we are out of alignment or being unduly influenced by the mad ideas of our ego and fear. It requires us to dig deeper and do the work to understand what is triggering us and why. With this knowledge, we then can access the wisdom that allows us to break free from our patterns and further our growth and actualization.

The final component of self-love, self-acceptance, is just that: acceptance. We must come to accept where we are and who we are, and choose to celebrate that, both the good and the bad. This is how we start down the path of growth and transformation.

IF YOU DON'T LOVE YOURSELF, YOU'LL END UP ABANDONING YOURSELF IN SERVICE OF OTHERS.

There is no guidebook to self-love—it's not a matter of following three easy steps and then you're done—because we all need different medicine. But ultimately the remedy is always the same: kindness, love, and empathy. For years I talked to myself and thought about myself in horrible ways. A negative and degrading track played over and over in my mind every time I looked at my reflection in the mirror or tried on a piece of clothing that didn't fit quite right. Self-love was the antidote to this self-loathing, shining light on the narrative, exposing the darkness, and addressing the fear.

We talk a lot about dispelling fear and lessening the impact of the ego in this book, but it is important to remember that fear and the ego serve a purpose. If they didn't, they wouldn't have such an outsized impact on us. On a primal level, their purpose is to keep us safe, as counter-intuitive as that might seem. In my case, the negative self-talk and body shaming was an effort to protect myself from the criticism of others. I thought that if anyone judged the way I looked, it would hurt less if I had already inflicted that pain upon myself. After all, they would be telling me what I already knew. It also kept me from putting myself in situations or environments that could potentially trigger those types of judgments. Everything we do, even if it harms us, we do for a reason.

Change, growth, and transformation take both time and effort, and sometimes we will fail and fall back into our old patterns. This is where self-love comes in. Instead of beating ourselves up when this happens, self-love allows us to acknowledge and recognize the detour, without judgment, and grant ourselves the grace of being in this process. What I have learned throughout my journey is that, first, there aren't as many people watching you as you think there are. Most aren't paying attention. They're too busy fighting their own demons and negative narratives. And second, those who are judgmental and hurtful don't actually mean to be. Their judgments are in fact moments of deflection, when they can't take another moment of their own self-judgment or self-criticism and instead deflect it onto others in an effort to relieve themselves temporarily from their self-inflicted suffering.

Self-love is about getting to the roots of what really hurts—

what you're trying to protect yourself from—and recognizing that you're safe. Beauty comes in myriad shapes, sizes, and colors. We distort our perceptions of ourselves based on what the media tells us we should look like, who we should be, and what is desirable. We build up these perceptions and then become tyrants in how we talk to and treat ourselves when we don't live up to these ideals. Self-love is about dismantling those ideals, and about being ok with where we are in our process and on our journey.

MIRRORS FOR BEAUTY

The Universe is constantly providing us mirrors for reflection. During my journey, I met a young man named John. I instantly felt a connection with him; he was ridiculously handsome, but his eyes hinted at a hidden tenderness and soft heart. Every time John received a compliment about how handsome he was, he brushed it off and countered that he was less than average. Which I found odd as that was usually my line. If you complimented his pictures, he would explain that it was a "good picture" and advise you to lower your expectations. Sometimes, he would follow up with a selfie that he claimed gave a more realistic likeness. Except both pictures looked exactly the same, no discernible difference. I began to ask myself what he was seeing that others weren't.

I encountered the same phenomenon with my friends. Every time we ran through photos I had shot, they needed to review the final selection, which I had already filtered, and veto the ones they didn't like. Except I could never understand why they didn't like certain pictures. They looked the same in all of them. All I could see was them. I began to ask myself if this was the same frustration that others had when

I dismissed my own pictures.

When we manufacture stories about our unlovability, our unworthiness, and our unattractiveness, they infuse the way we see ourselves. We focus on the parts of our bodies that we don't like or deem less than ideal. We concentrate on these parts of ourselves until that's all we see.

I've always believed that what people see is what we project. When someone feels confident and sexy, there is a noticeable difference in the way they carry themselves and show up in the world. But I've come to believe there is a caveat. God has created a fail-safe. One that allows others to see the beauty of God's divine creation, even when we don't see it ourselves. And so there is a lesson to take away from this.

When someone tells you how beautiful, amazing, attractive, pretty, or handsome you are, hear them. Hear them until you remember for yourself. Notice I use the word "remember," not "believe." You don't need to learn how to believe because deep down, you already do. Somewhere, buried deep, is the divine knowledge of exactly how magnificent you are. Over time, through the words of others and the stories you've made up about yourself, you may have forgotten. It's time to get out of your own way and remember. Let those around you help; listen to their words, their compliments, their praise. For they are doing God's work and recognizing the magnificence of his creation, even in the moments when you don't.

#LIGHTTALK

The journey of the Light Warrior is about reclaiming our worth. In order to do this, we need to first remove, or at least address, self-deprecation. Let's face it, none of us are perfect and we can all slip back into old patterns of thought and behavior, but that shouldn't deter us from trying to change. It is not what we do perfectly that has the power to transform our lives, but instead that which we practice consistently.

What are the areas in your life where you are hardest on yourself? Where do you carry the most self-judgment and self-criticism? Where do you feel that you fall short? What makes you tell yourself that you are not enough, or that you need to hustle to be worthy or accepted by others? When does your negative self-talk kick in? Is it constant, or is it triggered by certain situations? Is it your voice that you hear or the sound of someone you love? Often the negative talk we repeat to ourselves is an imprint left on us by a family member or friend. Self-love starts with self-compassion and self-awareness. This means being conscious of what is going on inside your mind, and how you're talking to yourself or treating yourself as a result. Often our negative self-talk expands to our actions, and we find ways to punish ourselves with workouts and strict diets, or by withholding love or isolating ourselves from others. How do your actions reflect your negative self-talk? Grab a pen and paper, and write them down.

Think about the negative narratives or the self-punishing behaviors you engage in. Freewrite about how each narrative or behavior serves you. What are you getting out of it? How does it protect you and keep you safe? What is it keeping you safe from? Take a few moments to answer these questions, allowing the words to flow onto the page without editing or rereading them. Let this process be free of judgment, allowing your thoughts and subconscious mind to take over and reveal what's hidden beneath the surface.

Lastly, ask yourself the following question: when did I first start feeling like I needed to protect myself from...? Use this as a cue to explore each of the behaviors you listed in the questions above. This might seem arduous, but it's imperative that we start to uncover the wounds that lie beneath these self-deprecating behaviors and narratives in order to heal them and begin the practice of self-love, of extending empathy towards ourselves and being kind. This practice is about developing a greater understanding of where our triggers lie and why they're there, if you can go that deep. It's part of the great work that we must do to self-actualize and become the best versions of ourselves. By stripping back the layers, and removing the masks that we put on over years of living in a world of labels and societal constructs, we reveal what was there all along.

Even if you struggle to recall the events that first led you to protect yourself, or what triggered your need to protect, becoming aware of the underlying patterns of your narratives and behaviors is a game changer. It allows us to reach deep inside during moments of self-attack and speak to our inner self or inner child with the same compassion and kindness we would use in speaking to a friend in pain. After all, that is where we are in these instances: in pain. Sometimes triggers aren't the result of pain but of fear—in some cases the fear of being happy or feeling joy. Dr. Brené Brown coined the term "foreboding joy". Joy is an intensely vulnerable emotion and often a scary one. Often we talk ourselves out of joy, imagining its end before we have even experienced it. We dress rehearse tragedy in order to protect ourselves from the pain and sadness we anticipate will follow, thereby robbing ourselves of experiencing joy in the present moment. Only later do we discover that of course we can never rehearse tragedy thoroughly enough to relieve us from the pain and sadness if and when it does strike.

We can learn to lean in to joy. It might be uncomfortable and scary at first, but it will get easier with time, as all practices do. We can begin by speaking kindly to ourselves and treating ourselves with compassion. We can recognize the journey we've taken, the hardships we've borne, and the commitment we've made to bettering our lives. We can recognize that we are deeply wounded and that instead of negative self-talk and self-deprecation, what we truly need is love, compassion, awareness, and acceptance. We can give ourselves the time and space to parent and nurture ourselves. Below is a Self-Love Meditation that I created during some of my most difficult moments in order to practice compassion and kindness towards myself. For a downloadable version of this meditation, visit: davidd.ca/warrior-tools.

SELF-LOVE MEDITATION

Sit quietly on the floor or in a chair with your feet planted firmly on the floor and your back straight.

Close your eyes.
Begin to breathe, slowly and deeply.
Breathing in, and breathing out.
Breathing in, breathing out.

Bring your hands together in prayer at the center of your chest.

Palms facing each other and gently touching.
Breathing in, and breathing out.
Breathing in, breathing out.

Begin to rub your hands together.
Allowing the friction and momentum to build.
Breathing in, and breathing out.

Breathing in, breathing out.

Slowly begin to increase the pace,
Rubbing your hands together a little faster.
Continue to breathe.
Breathing in, and breathing out.
Breathing in, breathing out.

Go a little faster now.
Feeling the heat beginning to rise between your palms.
Continuing to allow the energy to build between your hands.

Breathing in, and breathing out.
Breathing in, breathing out.

On the next inhale, stop rubbing your hands together and hold them in prayer at your chest.

As you exhale, slowly pull your palms apart, just by a few inches.

Feel the energy between your palms as you slowly move your hands towards each other and then further apart.

Let your fingers tingle. Continue to breathe as you play with this sensation.

Breathing in, and breathing out.

Turn your hands so that both palms are facing your chest, and gently place them over your heart.

Breathe into the energy you have just raised.

Marinate in this feeling.

Repeating to yourself:
I love you.
I love you.
I love you.

Breathing in, and breathing out.

Breathing in, breathing out.

I love you.
I love you.
I love you.

I'm sorry for how hard I am on you.
For not allowing you to shine.
For not allowing you to step into the greatness of all that you could be.

I love you.
I love you.
I love you.

Breathing in, and breathing out.
Breathing in, breathing out.

I love you.
I love you.
I love you.

You are worthy.
You are worthy of love and belonging.
You are enough.
You are enough, just as you are.
Perfectly imperfect.

I love you.
I love you.
I love you.

Continue to marinate in this energy.
Breathing in, and breathing out.
Breathing in, breathing out.

Repeat to yourself:
I love you.
I love you.
I love you.

When you're ready, take a few moments to settle back into your body, gentling wiggling your fingers and toes.

Take another deep breath in and, when you're ready, open your eyes to the room.

EGO WILL TELL US WE ARE BEING TESTED.

THESE ARE
THE WOUNDS
LEFT TO BE
HEALED.

CHAPTER 9

WHEN YOU'VE DONE THE WORK

ALL CHANGE IS HARD AT FIRST, MESSY IN THE MIDDLE AND GORGEOUS AT THE END.
—ROBIN SHARMA, *THE 5AM CLUB*

DOES THE WORK BRING THE TRIALS?

In the early half of 2017, once I had gotten settled into my new place and my father had made a full recovery, I decided it was time to put myself back out there. That is, it was time to start dating again. I felt ready. But, to my surprise and frustration, I kept attracting more of the same: men who were highly promiscuous and unfaithful or men with drug and consumption problems (not hardcore drugs, but certainly alcohol and marijuana addictions). I looked back on the past decade and thought to myself, "Haven't we been here before?" I had done the work. Why did it feel like I was back where I started? Was I being tested?

The idea of God testing us was a notion I had grown up with, and one that I had heard often in my life, but it never really resonated with me. It just didn't feel right. A kind and compassionate God, or Universe, wouldn't do something so trivial and petty as testing us to determine whether we would give in to temptation or fall into familiar patterns. I wasn't buying it.

But if it wasn't a test, why was this happening? I thought back to the idea of easy buttons. One thing that was clear to me was destructive patterns around sex, alcohol, and drugs were ways to escape burdens and pain. But why did people with these sorts of patterns keep being brought into my life? For a short while, I believed it was so I could help heal them. If I'm being truly honest, I thought my role was to save them. That illusion quickly dissipated when I broached the subject with a person I was dating at the time who wasn't receptive to it in the least. I was stumped. If I wasn't supposed to help them, then it had to mean they were in my life for a reason. But for the life of me, I couldn't understand what they were supposed to teach me. I had been down this path before; I knew this wasn't what I wanted in my life. Wasn't that knowledge enough? Why was I back here again?

Late one afternoon, while I was showering after a particularly defeating day, I figured it out. It was because I hadn't yet learned to say "no" to what I didn't want. I had achieved a level of awareness of what I wanted, but I hadn't learned how to vocalize it and declare my desires. Before I got married, I had seen most of the red flags that would ultimately destroy our union, but I had kept quiet. I had turned a blind eye, thinking that if I spoke up and said, "no," to this person or relationship, another might not come around and I would end up alone.

Clearly, I still had some internal wounds that needed healing. My belief that I wasn't worthy of more was keeping me in relationships that weren't aligned with what I wanted. They would eventually dissolve on their own when I became so uninterested in these destructive behaviors that I would disengage. This might sound like an ideal way to avoid dealing with wounds and issues, but I can assure you it's not. I was losing months and years of my life in the process, time that could never be recuperated.

Red flags were usually present right from the first date but, even after I saw them, I would still always move forward. I would tell myself that perhaps it was just a false reading; maybe they were nervous or trying to seem popular or cool. After all, getting drunk and high was trendy and glamorized in the media, and everyone just wants to be accepted. I reassured myself that, by the second date, their nerves would settle down and the real person would emerge. Secretly, I thought maybe, just maybe, this relationship would be a pivotal moment in their lives and break old habits. Yes, I still had some residual savior syndrome left. I wanted so much to see the inherent good in people because I knew it was there. I didn't regret that impulse; in fact, I was grateful for it. It may come across as naïveté, but I would much prefer that to cynicism. But, as a result, whenever these issues came up, I either kept quiet or pretended like they didn't bother me. Oh, you like to smoke up? No, that doesn't bother me. It's your body, not mine. Oh, you don't want kids? To be honest, I'm not sure I do either. I've been back and forth. Why was I hiding from what I knew was my truth? Was I that scared that there weren't other fish in the sea?

Reflecting on my answers, I realized that the behaviors and scripts I employed were those of someone who lacks self-worth. Here is an example of my internal dialogue. You may be familiar with some of this.

> I won't ask for what I want or speak up about what I don't because I don't deserve it.
> I'm afraid that if I speak up, I won't get what I want, which will prove that I didn't deserve it.
> I'm afraid that if I speak up, I'll be misunderstood or perceived the wrong way, and people will judge me or leave.

I'm afraid that if I speak up and they leave, it will prove that my fear was right and that I didn't deserve anything better.

Ultimately there is no path that gets us to what we want when we think we aren't worthy. That was the lesson these experiences were meant to show me. I wasn't being tested. I was being shown what was left to do to heal. It was an acknowledgment of all the work I had done. Now I was on the last leg of the journey that would allow me to finally move forward. Awareness was the biggest part of the process because you can't change what you can't name. Being aware of the pattern is half the battle. But then you must act on that awareness. Speaking up and saying no to what you don't want isn't always easy. I can attest to that. But it's a practice and a muscle that becomes stronger the more you train it. Every time we say no, or we speak our truth, it becomes a little easier to do so the next time.

BOUNDARIES: HOLD THE LINE, DON'T DRAW A NEW ONE

One of the lessons that emerged when I began dating again was just how much I sucked at establishing and upholding boundaries. I had certainly seen that over the course of my marriage. Every time a line was crossed, I'd take a step back and draw a new line. Why? I had already established that infidelity wasn't acceptable. Why did I tolerate having that line crossed again and again? Was it because I didn't believe that I was worthy of more? Worthy of love and respect? This had become a recurring problem. Why was it so easy for people to cross my boundaries? One of the reasons was clearly that I wasn't upholding them. That much I knew. But why didn't people even recognize or acknowledge they were there? I could see where other people's boundaries lay, even if they were silent or unspoken boundaries, so why were others so willing to ignore and cross mine?

> **WHEN WE FAIL TO SET BOUNDARIES AND HOLD PEOPLE ACCOUNTABLE, WE FEEL USED AND MISTREATED. THIS IS WHY WE SOMETIMES ATTACK WHO THEY ARE, WHICH IS FAR MORE HURTFUL THAN ADDRESSING A BEHAVIOR OR A CHOICE.**
> —BRENÉ BROWN, *THE GIFTS OF IMPERFECTION: LET GO OF WHO YOU THINK YOU'RE SUPPOSED TO BE AND EMBRACE WHO YOU ARE*

Every time another one of my boundaries would fall, I would find myself in an almost panicked state. Lines had been crossed, sacred space had been trespassed, and now the threat of pain and being hurt was real again. Boundaries can't keep us safe from everything, but they're meant to be the gate that controls what come in and out.

One such instance occurred in the spring of 2018. My ex-husband and I had been separated and living apart for two years. During that time, there had been next to no communication aside from the occasional message to coordinate signing and submitting divorce papers. Life was good, and I was content with him not being a part of my life anymore. I no longer held any grudges or resentment towards him; that chapter had come to an end, and I was writing the next chapter of my life.

Then one morning he texted to ask if he could borrow my circular saw to cut wood for a project he was doing. I had kept the saw because it was a gift from my dad. My instant reaction was to respond and say, "Sure," not because I was listening to my gut or my intuition, but simply because I have a knee-jerk reaction to please and be accommodating. He responded immediately, thanking me and letting me know that he would come by in the evening to pick it up. Immediately, my stomach turned to knots. I hadn't thought through the possibility that he intended to come over and pick it up, and that I would actually need to see him in order for the exchange to take place. I knew instantly that I didn't really want to see him, and certainly wasn't comfortable letting him into my home. I had worked hard to create a new home for myself, one where the energy was peaceful and inviting. I considered it sacred—still do—and, as such, I had become extremely mindful about who I let enter my space. No arguments, no foul words or name-calling, had transpired between these walls. The only things that had been cultivated in this space were love and joy.

Now my intuition was speaking to me and I was listening. This wasn't a good idea. To make matters worse, he wanted to come that evening, which would mean skipping my scheduled yoga class. Not a huge deal, but for me it meant sacrificing my own needs and plans in order to accommodate someone else, someone who I no longer had a relationship with or any obligation towards. I wanted to get out of the whole situation, but I felt the need to look for some middle ground, especially since I had already said yes before giving it much thought. I responded that tonight wouldn't work and that I was busy most of the week, but I could drop the saw off at his office. His office was close to mine and going there wouldn't require much of a detour from my regular commute. I figured this would save him from having to transport a bulky piece of equipment on public transit since I lived outside the city and he didn't have a car. He wrote back that my plan wouldn't work and that he would come pick up the saw at my place the following night and take a taxi home.

I felt my body start to shake. How was I going to get out of this? I called my soul sister Lara and explained the situation. I told her he was insisting on coming over and picking it up, and I didn't want him in my home. I had closed that door a long time ago and wasn't willing to reopen it. She was quiet on the other end of the line as I rambled in my panicked state. When I was done, she reminded me of all the boundary work I had done and taught. I took a deep breath. She was right. If this wasn't ok, it was my responsibility to vocalize that and uphold my boundaries. I was reminded in that moment that God works through people. Lara reminded me that just because someone was a part of your life at one time doesn't mean they will always be. We had severed our relationship and gone down different paths, and that was ok. Those paths didn't need to reconnect if I didn't wish them to. It was exactly what I needed to hear.

Responding to my ex-husband, I explained that him coming over to pick it up wouldn't work for me and that us seeing each other wasn't the best idea. I apologized for having committed to lending the saw before giving it much thought. I advised him that there was a hardware shop a few blocks from his apartment. I had called ahead and they had circular saws in stock and rented them by the day, which would end up costing him less than the taxi to and from the suburbs and save him time as well. He insisted, asking if he could pick it up from my parents' place so that we wouldn't need to see each other. He didn't want to spend money on the rental as he had recently stopped working. I apologized and said that that wouldn't be possible either; if money was a concern, then the proposed solution would be the most cost-effective.

My hands shook with every message I read and every reply I sent but, when it was over, I felt as though a weight had been lifted. I had held my boundaries, gracefully, and stayed true to my beliefs and integrity.

MATTERS OF PRINCIPLE

We often blur the lines between our principles and values. Our values guide our lives, the decisions we make, the people we choose to surround ourselves with, the way we choose to show up in the world. Our principles, on the other hand, guide our behaviors. Sometimes our principles become disconnected from our values. When life gets hard and we find ourselves backed into a corner, this is usually because we are using the wrong compass to guide ourselves. Principles should be the manifestation of our values; they are downstream from our beliefs.

Among my values are loyalty and integrity. Loyalty is a value passed down to me from my father; integrity is one I was born with. By integrity, I mean being honest and having strong principles, and being complete and integral in how I show up in the world. Part of my integrity is understanding the weight of my words and commitments that I make. I stayed in my marriage for years not because of my values, but because of my principles. My values had been violated, first by my husband, and then by myself when I chose to stay in an environment that robbed me of those values. I stayed out of a matter of principle (among other things). I had made a commitment, and I had made vows. My values no longer supported those decisions, but I held tightly to my principles out of fear that, if I let go, I would lose sight of my values. In fact, the opposite happened: I lost sight of my values because I clung too tightly to my principles, not seeing the forest for the trees.

Our principles can imprison us if we cling to them too tightly. It is important to remember that our principles are simply the day-to-day manifestations of our values. They are the ways in which we choose to express our values to the world. This means they can change. There are a million ways to be loyal or to show integrity. We can loosen our grip on our principles and let our values take the wheel, showing us a different way to be in the world that will not rob us of ourselves.

When our principles begin to cage us or rob us of joy, it's time to discard them. Put them aside and look to the sky, finding your north. These are your values. Ask yourself where they would have you go.

#LIGHTTALK

This chapter is about becoming aware of and examining the patterns that continue to present themselves even as we do the work and start the healing. Our ego might tell us that we are being tested or that we haven't worked hard enough. It will seek any readily available evidence to make us believe this is so. Instead we should see in these patterns the areas that are left unhealed and the work that is left to be done in order to move forward. This is our opportunity to get curious. What keeps showing up? What fears keep coming back around? What still requires healing or release?

During this stage in my journey, I was forced to recognize that not everyone who entered my life was there to be guided, saved, or healed. We are all responsible for our own healing; no one can do that for us. Guides will show up when we are ready, but they cannot do our work. We have free will, and it is our decision to walk the path of the Warrior. This requires putting in the work, healing our wounds, and moving into a new way of being.

One challenge faced by many people I've worked with, especially women (although this applies to men as well; I'm certainly proof of that), is setting boundaries. Our ego would have us believe that establishing boundaries pushes people away, causing us to be disliked or rejected. Among our basic core needs are the needs for connection and belonging. Anything that could potentially threaten those needs is scary business. But establishing boundaries allows us to show others the ways in which we care for and respect ourselves. This, in turn, demonstrates the ways in which we are able to care for and respect others. We can set boundaries with grace.

Most people are good at knowing where their boundaries lie, or at least become cognizant of them once they have been crossed. It invokes a feeling in the pit of your stomach—some would call it rage. However it manifests, it is an emotional reaction to the fact that an injustice has occurred and something you hold dear has been violated. The intensity of our emotional response is directly corelated to the number of times that boundary has been crossed. However, we often override that reaction, and many of us—especially us people-pleasing folks—just take a step back and draw a new line. The problem is that each time we do this, our reactions become more explosive and aggressive, and eventually we find ourselves on the edge of a metaphorical cliff. Another step back and we will lose ourselves completely. Then we are forced to push forward hard because now our survival depends on it. But it doesn't have to be this way.

Instead, we can practice keeping our boundaries with grace. We start by asking the intruder or violator to take a step back and clarifying that a boundary has been crossed. This can be done kindly and compassionately, as I did with my ex-husband. Then we may want to explain and communicate why that boundary is there. This explanation is not always necessary. Not all of our decisions require justification to others, but explaining ourselves is a deep form of compassion towards ourselves and others. When I needed to reestablish boundaries with my ex-husband, I explained that the wounds and pain from our time together still ran deep and that it was difficult and painful to be around each other. This permitted me to practice compassion, not only with myself, but with him as well.

If someone is being rude or disrespectful, or using curse words, it is ok to establish or communicate an existing boundary by saying, "I'm sorry, but for me to continue this conversation with you, I'm going to need you to refrain from cursing (or being vulgar or disrespectful)." It might feel awkward or clumsy at first, but it gets easier the more we practice it. If situations repeatedly present themselves where this is necessary, it may be worthwhile to practice these conversations on your own.

The second step, after communicating your boundaries, is upholding them. This may require you to reiterate that you already communicated your boundary and extract yourself from this situation/conversation. You may want to suggest that you pick this up at a later date/time, or you may not. Resist the urge to succumb to please others, violating your own needs in the process.

It's worth noting that there are unspoken boundaries that exist for all of us. These are basic human rights and needs. For example, we all have the right to be treated with respect and humanity. Regardless of whether someone vocalizes boundaries around these fundamental rights and needs, it is important to always remember they are present and universal. Respecting and upholding these for ourselves and others is a moral responsibility and part of being a Light Warrior.

REFLECTION EXERCISE

Take some time to reflect on the work you've done. Who have you been practicing forgiveness towards? Have you been forgiving yourself? What are the areas of your life that still hurt and cause you pain and frustration despite the work you've done? How do these patterns, situations, and relationships continue to manifest and show up in your life? Take some time to freewrite, letting your words and thoughts flow fluidly without censorship or judgment. Explore what's still coming up for you that you need to release and heal.

How is your ego contributing to these situations? Is part of your frustration or resistance because you believe these areas of your life should look differently? Perhaps they should, but are you holding too tightly to a particular ideal, inhibiting room for the Universe to manifest something truly worthy of you? Sometimes these ideals need to be released and let go so that you can properly mourn and heal.

Allow yourself some time to sit in meditation and release these areas of your life to your higher power. Ask for healing and to be guided to the next right step, to further your journey and finally allow you to move beyond these situations and this pain. Trust that your prayers will always be answered even if the insight or answer doesn't occur immediately. Remain open and ready to receive the answer you seek in the hours and days to follow. Remember that God and the Universe work through people and you may find yourself in the presence of someone who will tell you about a book you need to read, or an individual you need to meet or speak with, or perhaps will themselves say the words that will guide you to the next steps of your healing.

OUR WORTH IS INHERENT. WE ARE

BORN
WORTHY AND
THAT NEVER
CHANGES.

CHAPTER 10

EVERY IDEA HAS ITS DAWN

> WE DO NOT BELIEVE IN OURSELVES UNTIL SOMEONE REVEALS THAT DEEP INSIDE US SOMETHING IS VALUABLE, WORTH LISTENING TO, WORTHY OF OUR TRUST, SACRED TO OUR TOUCH. ONCE WE BELIEVE IN OURSELVES WE CAN RISK CURIOSITY, WONDER, SPONTANEOUS DELIGHT OR ANY EXPERIENCE THAT REVEALS THE HUMAN SPIRIT.
> —E.E. CUMMINGS

OUR WORTH IS INHERENT

As I continued down my path of healing and self-discovery, one underlying thread seemed to connect everything I learned and encountered. Self-worth. The upsetting irony was I didn't think I possessed any. But there it was, at the heart of everything. The reason I stayed in bad relationships and continued to attract new ones. The reason I kept saying yes to people who chose me (because I didn't feel I was worthy enough to choose for myself). The reason I had so much difficulty upholding boundaries and saying no to what I didn't want in my life. I had stayed in a marriage riddled with infidelity and lies because I didn't believe I was worthy of more or that I deserved better. I had finally left when the pain and suffering became unbearable, but my decision to pursue a better life wasn't based on a proper foundation of self-worth; it was about survival. Clearly, finding my sense of self-worth would be a crucial part of my journey.

There is a difference between being worthy and being deserving. Our worth is inherent. We are born worthy and that never changes. We are always, every moment of our lives, worthy of love, belonging, connection, empathy, and joy. Whether or not we believe we deserve these things is inconsequential to our worth. Our worth stems from the divine spark that lies within us—our humanity, our innocence, our love. This spark was not born of us—we didn't create it and as such we can't destroy, diminish, or alter it. It cannot be taken or given away.

There are times when we may forget these truths. We may choose to forget that we are worthy. By placing our hands over our eyes, we may try to pretend we were born without self-worth or have lost it because of some decision we have made that we perceive to be bad. We do this by buying into and believing the stories we make up about ourselves that diminish our inherent worth. In these moments, it is important to remember that none of us are perfect and we've all done wrong at one point or another, or proceeded down the wrong path even though we knew better. We may have, as a result, intentionally or unintentionally, caused harm to others or ourselves. This truth has no impact on our worth and doesn't make us any less deserving of forgiveness, provided we practice atonement. When we atone, we recognize that we acted out of alignment with our truth and forgot who we are, perhaps driven by fear. Atoning does not require lavish gestures or acts of self-flagellation, whether it be emotional, physical, or mental. Atonement is an essential part of self-forgiveness. It is the acknowledgement that we weren't within our right mind and may have acted under the influence of our ego or fear. This acknowledgment allows us to hand the situation over to something greater than ourselves, perhaps a higher power, so that it can be corrected. The third step of atonement is simply being open to where you will be led as a result of this acknowledgement. Sometimes apologies are necessary so that forgiveness and healing may occur and compassion practiced.

When we believe we aren't worthy or lack worth, we seek experiences, jobs, titles, possessions, and relationships that will define our worth for us. We seek validation from the outside world to bolster our sense of self-worth. But there is no one person and thing out there that can define your worth for you. I can't sit here and tell you your worth. I can simply tell you you are worthy. The only person who can define your worth is you. Only you know the journey and the path you have taken to be here. Only you know the demons you have slayed and the distances you have traveled.

Most people occasionally struggle with issues of self-worth. I consider this struggle part of the human condition. The outside world is constantly telling us who and what we should be and that, if we don't measure up or conform to social standards and stereotypes, we simply aren't good enough. Asking others to validate or define your worth when they are most likely struggling with understanding and believing their own is a losing game. I often refer to the metaphor of a shopper bargaining at a flea market. They will only be willing to pay as much as they have in their pocket, and rare is the shopper who is so sure of their find that they are willing to pay every cent they have. Similarly, asking others to define our worth, when their account is already at a deficit, becomes a negotiation, looking for middle ground.

There is no middle ground as it relates to our worth. We are worthy of all of it.

When we choose to believe that we are unworthy, we give away our power. This includes our power to affect any form of change in our world and the world of others. *A Course In Miracles* explains that we are all connected. Choosing to believe that we are separate from one another is like a sunbeam choosing to believe it is separate from other sunbeams. Or a wave in the ocean believing that it is separate from other waves. We are all connected through our humanity and through our divinity. We are part of a collective consciousness and, when we choose to believe that we are unworthy, we pollute that shared consciousness. This muddies the waters for others and makes it easier for them to opt out of who they truly are. And so it is imperative that we remember our worth and reclaim it. It never left us. It never got smaller or changed. We simply forgot it was there. It's time we remove our hands from our eyes.

WHEN THE EGO TAKES THE WHEEL

What I remember most vividly about trying my hand at dating after my separation was not the dates or the people I met, but the narrative that went on in my mind and the physical traumas I experienced in my body. I had done a lot of work on restoring and reclaiming my self-worth, but dating exposed the work that was left to do. I didn't trust easily, and my ego, which had long compiled evidence that I was unworthy, was eager to collect more.

Here's the thing about the ego: it is constantly searching for evidence to make our fears appear real. Neal Donald Walsh coined the acronym "F.E.A.R.", which stands for "false evidence appearing real." Our ego looks for evidence that would further anchor our belief in it, not because it wants to be a detrimental force of destruction or evil in our lives, but because this is how it tries to keep us safe. It reminds us of our fears in order to keep us from entering situations that could potentially cause us harm. Our evolution, expansion, and enlightenment will always trigger the amygdala, our fear-based mind, because these propel us into new situations and environments. Change is unsafe, at least for the ego. The further we get on our path, the closer we get to our transformation or healing, the louder the ego will speak in an attempt to derail our efforts and keep us small and safe. But we aren't living in primitive times, and our fears don't represent the dangers they once did. Our world has evolved and changed, but the nature and purpose of the ego has not. Fear keeps us from walking down dark alleys or speeding on a freeway, but it also keeps us from changing. The dangers of meeting new people and entering new social situations aren't that real at all.

Love, on the other hand, never looks for evidence. *A Course In Miracles* can be summarized in the following words.

ONLY LOVE IS REAL.
NOTHING UNREAL EXISTS.
HEREIN LIES THE PEACE OF GOD.

Love doesn't need evidence because it is all that is. We, on the other hand, sometimes need to search for spiritual proof in order to tame or quiet the voice of the ego and keep it from taking the wheel.

Whenever I would meet someone new, the beginning was always exciting. The calls and messages, getting to know each other. Then there would be a moment when there was a gap in communications: a message wasn't responded to, a call wasn't answered, or a voicemail went unreturned. This would cause my ego to swing into full gear. Why weren't they calling me back? Why hadn't they responded to my message? Why had things gone quiet? I assumed they had seen me for who I was now and realized that I wasn't enough—not good enough, smart enough, successful enough, handsome enough, etc. My mind would spin out of control, leading me down the rabbit hole until I was so engulfed by my thoughts and narratives that I could barely function. I share this because I know I'm not alone in this experience.

In those moments of panic, I learned to turn to my spiritual toolbox. I would meditate, freewrite, or call up a friend to shed light on my shame. When all else failed, I would turn to the Ego Eradicator Meditation, which I'll share at the end of this chapter.

On one such occasion, I sat down to meditate to stop the chaos of my mind and ego, and heard the words of Yogi Bhajan once again.

THE OTHER PERSON IS YOU.

I had been struggling for days to calm my ego but, when these words came through, I found a sense of peace begin to set in. I had been mystified by how attractive the person I was dating was, and part of me (my ego) couldn't believe someone like that would be interested in someone like me. Surely, they hadn't truly seen me, I thought, despite having met on more than one occasion. My ego had me convinced they must have made a mistake and that it would only be a matter of time before they woke up. But Yogi Bhajan's words reminded me that we all have our struggles. Eventually, I realized that, while I was struggling over my physical appearance and the fear of not measuring up, this person was struggling with something else and believed they too didn't measure up and would be found out. Once we were able to put our fears aside, we were able to see that we weren't actually compatible—not because any of our fear-based thoughts were true, because they weren't, but because we wanted vastly different things for our lives and futures.

That is the beauty of releasing our fear and reconnecting to our worth. It allows us to hold space for each other and see each other through the lens of love and compassion. In this way, reclaiming our worth is the most important thing we can do to make an impact on the lives of the people around us. Because it changes the filter through which we view the world. When we release our fears and the mad thoughts of the ego, we can see how we are all connected and that our struggles aren't ours alone. They are part of this human experience and allow us to bear witness to how many people are calling out for love, no matter how obscured the message they are sending may be.

> **THE ONLY REASON WE DON'T OPEN OUR HEARTS AND MINDS TO OTHER PEOPLE IS THAT THEY TRIGGER CONFUSION IN US THAT WE DON'T FEEL BRAVE ENOUGH OR SANE ENOUGH TO DEAL WITH. TO THE DEGREE THAT WE LOOK CLEARLY AND COMPASSIONATELY AT OURSELVES, WE FEEL CONFIDENT AND FEARLESS ABOUT LOOKING INTO SOMEONE ELSE'S EYES.**
> —PEMA CHÖDRÖN, *WHEN THINGS FALL APART: HEART ADVICE FOR DIFFICULT TIMES*

RELATIONSHIPS & WANTING MORE

Here are a few things I've learned on this journey. As Maya Angelou said in a quote I shared at the beginning of this book, "When someone shows you who they are, believe them." When the red flags appear, believe them. Don't turn a blind eye and fall in love with the potential of a person or a relationship. You'll end up feeling like you're pushing a rock up a hill. The only potential you should concern yourself with is your own. To realize potential requires desire and ambition; you can only do this for yourself. Growing into who we want to be is a personal journey, but more importantly it's a personal choice. Not everyone will decide to embark on that journey; that doesn't mean that they are wrong or less evolved. It means that their work in this lifetime may be different.

It is a Buddhist and Hindu belief that the path to enlightenment spans many lifetimes and that we enter each life with a path set before us to take us on the next part of our journey—a lesson plan or sacred contract, if you will. Each person's path to enlightenment is different; the lessons others are here to face and learn from may not be the same as what you want for them. Pushing someone into a better job or career, or a relationship, or family life because of their and your potential may not be aligned with their path. Just as continuous striving may not be aligned with yours. We push ourselves and others forward with the hopes that it will increase our worth. But this is a misunderstanding of how worth works.

When we strip back all the layers—the cars, houses, jobs, titles, spouses, money—what is left? Who are we? When we ask ourselves who we are based on the value we provide to the world, just by showing up as our true selves and contributing our unique strengths, we begin to understand the inherent worth we were born with, and suddenly the materials things don't seem to matter as much. Life becomes less about status and more about presence. When we are clear about our worth, the threat of success or failure melt away, and instead we can immerse ourselves in the joy of doing and creating. Trying to live up to the expectations others set for you or that society has defined for you is exhausting and highly depleting. Living with the knowledge of your worth outside of those material measures is empowering and energizing.

In most spiritual circles that preach gratitude, wanting more is deemed unspiritual or unenlightened. I tend to disagree depending on where the need for more stems from. There is something to be said for healthy striving, a desire to learn and grow and be better today than we were yesterday. But if your hustle is purely attached to who you will become once you achieve whatever it is you're after, then it's time to get curious. What limiting belief are you holding onto that is attaching your self-worth to the hustle? If our desire for more is because we've attached our worth and who we are to what we have, then we still have work to do.

We are spiritual beings living in a material world. Wanting more for the future and setting our sights on goals or plans doesn't have to detract from the gratitude we can have in the present moment for all that we have and the blessings that have been bestowed upon us. Sometime wanting more also means we get to provide more and give back more. For entrepreneurs, wanting more—more clients, more business, more income—means that they can also give back more. For example, by contributing towards charitable and philanthropic initiatives. As parents, wanting more—for example, a bigger house—means being able to have a bigger family. Perhaps it means being able to adopt children and provide a home or a chance at a better future. What is your wanting more in service of? Do you want more just because you want more? Is it because you are comparing yourself to others? What does it contribute to: your well-being or the well-being of others? There is nothing wrong with wanting more, provided we aren't attaching who are to what we want and believing that what we have, accomplish, or attain will make us enough.

#LIGHTTALK

Reclaiming our self-worth is the fastest path to raising our vibrations and changing our lives. It all comes from the principle and core belief that you were born worthy. Nothing you will ever do in this lifetime will change that.

YOU WERE BORN. YOU'RE HERE. YOU'RE BREATHING. YOU'RE WORTHY.

The reason reclaiming our worth is so important is because it directly correlates to how we show up in the world. It affects our presence, our impact, and most importantly our message. You don't need to be taking a political, environmental, or social stand to have a message. What's in your heart? What's important to you? That's your message. You're here to spread love in your own unique way, to be a beacon of light for yourself and others; that is the path of the Warrior. What takes us out of alignment and separates us from our worth are the mad ideas of the ego: that we are less than, that others are better, further along, or more worthy than we are. We easily accept these beliefs because our perceptions of ourselves are often distorted. Because we seek light and desire to embody it and become beacons for those around us, we believe that, every time we fail or resort to judgment or give into our fear, we give away our light. But it is precisely because of this that we are Light Warriors. Because when we fail, when we stumble, we get back up and continue our pursuit of light, love, truth, and compassion.

In the early days of stumbling my way through this work, I knew very little of who I truly was, what my potential was, or what I was worth. I simply knew that there was more to life than what I had been living. I felt sure that I had been put here for a reason. The events of my life so far may have been a part of my narrative, but the ending wasn't written yet. I wasn't my narrative; it was just a story of what had happened to me. It didn't need to define me.

> What stories do you tell about yourself? How much of how you think of yourself and your worth do you attach to them? Are you a martyr, or the helpless victim? Were you cheated on or abused? Did you receive a diagnosis? When you tell yourself or other people your story, are these things just events that happened to you or are they how you define yourself?

As I was beginning to emerge from my narrative, I reached out to a group of friends, people I knew well and trusted, whom I knew truly saw me for who I was. I asked them to pick out a few words that described me. If I was a superhero, these would be my superpowers. My inbox was flooded with messages. Many of the same words appeared over and over again. For the first time, I saw a glimpse of myself as others saw me. None of the character faults or imperfections that I had been focusing on made the list. While those words don't encompass all of who I am, because I get to choose who I am and who I will be, they make up a part of the whole. And when I'm feeling down, or my ego has me trapped in a story of separation and unworthiness, those words serve as a gentle reminder. If you asked the same question to those who love you, what would they say? What words would they use?

In those moments when you are feeling stuck or unworthy, here are some tools to help you realign. First, reach out to a friend or spiritual running buddy, someone who can bring in some light and truly knows you and sees you for the beautiful and amazing soul that you are. Use them as a mirror so that you can catch a glimpse of your own light. After all, that is what we truly do for each other: hold up mirrors so that we can allow each other to truly see our wounds, our desires, our beliefs—both beautiful and limiting—and, most importantly, our light. When you see light in someone else, remind yourself that it is a reflection of your own, because that light dwells within each of us.

Second, reach out and be of service to someone. Find someone you can interact with and extend some love and compassion towards. Who do you know who is suffering and would appreciate a call? This interaction doesn't need to involve you guiding them or giving them advice; we help others just by being present and listening with both our ears and our heart. Help a stranger cross the street or carry their bags. Give someone a smile. Offer the person ahead of you in line at Starbucks a compliment; it may be the nicest thing they hear all day. Drop blessings wherever you go. Pray that any who enter this space be blessed with peace and their heart's desire while in line at the ATM or sitting on the bus. There is nothing that pulls us out of our slumps faster than being of service to others. It allows us to reconnect to our inherent nature.

IF YOU ARE FEELING HELPLESS, HELP SOMEONE.
—AUNG SAN SUU KYI

Lastly, use the Ego Eradicator Meditation at the end of this chapter. Often the effects of our fear and the ideas and thoughts of the ego manifest themselves in the body, creating energy blocks that can cause us to feel drained, sad, depressed, and lethargic. Over time, this can culminate and manifest in sickness or disease. Use this meditation to clear these energy blocks from the body and provide you with mental clarity, bringing the false ideologies of the ego to the light so that they can be dissolved.

EGO ERADICATOR MEDITATION

The best way I have found to clear my mind when stuck in a whirlwind of thoughts, emotions, and fear is by using the Ego Eradicator Meditation. Ego Eradicator is a kundalini yoga meditation composed of a particular mudra (hand position) and breathing technique called Kapalabhati (Breath of Fire).

Start by placing your hands on your belly. Feel how your belly protrudes and extends as you inhale, and retreats and collapses back towards the spine as you exhale. If you're not accustomed to deep belly breathing, start by practicing it first. Most of us have become accustomed to shallow breathing into our chest, especially those of us concerned with body image and trying to keep our core tight at all times. I know because I used to be one of those people.

Once you are comfortable with this type of deep breathing, you are ready to practice Breath of Fire. Begin in the same fashion by placing your hand on your belly. Take a deep breath in through your nose with your mouth closed but, on the exhale, breathe out only a short burst of air through your nose and take another short breath in through your nose. Keep repeating this short breathing cycle, allowing your belly to move in unison with your breath, rhythmically like the beating of a drum. Do not inverse the motion of your belly, expanding on the exhale and contracting on the inhale, as this can restrict airflow and cause you to become light-headed or even pass out.

Note: Breath of Fire should not be practiced if you are pregnant or suffering from a medical condition without first consulting with a medical professional.

To perform Ego Eradicator, sit on the floor, legs crossed or in Sukhasana (Easy Pose), or in a chair with your back straight and your feet planted firmly on the floor. With your eyes closed, breathe slowly and deeply. You can choose to perform this meditation in complete silence or to a piece of rhythmic music.

Hold your arms straight above your head, fingertips pointing upwards. Extend your thumbs out to the sides so that they are perpendicular to your palm and the tips of both thumbs are touching each other. Curl your index, middle, ring, and pinkie fingers into the palms of your hand so that your hands resemble a thumbs up or hitchhiking position. Now lower your arms to each side slightly so that they are at a 45° angle and your hands are still above the top of your head. Begin Breath of Fire, holding your arms out to either side.

Let your thoughts clear as you focus on your breathing. Perform this meditation for 3-5 minutes, allowing it to remove the blocks of fear and your ego, and clear your body of any stagnant energy.

When you are done, bring your arms back over your head, touching your thumbs together. Take a deep breath in, and as you exhale bring your hands down to prayer in the center of your chest.

When you're ready, open your eyes to the room.

For guided meditations to support you through Breath of Fire and Ego Eradicator, visit davidd.ca/warrior-tools

SOMETIMES THE MOST LOVING

RESPONSES ARE SETTING BOUNDARIES.

CHAPTER 11

FINDING TRUTH

**AT THE CENTER OF YOUR BEING
YOU HAVE THE ANSWER;
YOU KNOW WHO YOU ARE
AND YOU KNOW WHAT YOU WANT.**
—LAO TZU

I believe we all encounter many truths over the course of our lives that bring us closer to one ultimate truth. It may take many lifetimes and journeys to reach that ultimate truth, but each small truth brings us closer to an understanding of the intricate workings of our Universe and our Creator. These are some of the truths I encountered in my journey.

**THE KNOWLEDGE THAT ILLUMINATES NOT
ONLY SETS YOU FREE, BUT ALSO SHOWS YOU
CLEARLY THAT YOU ARE FREE.**
—*A COURSE IN MIRACLES*

MY BIGGEST HEALER & TEACHER

I have talked a lot over the course of my coaching and in this book about the events of my marriage and the challenges I encountered. Truth be told, some counseled me against this and inquired why I would choose to share so much. I also realize that by sharing my story, I have had to inadvertently expose someone else's. But it was always my intention to be truthful in the telling of my story and to focus on my experience of marriage and the challenges of infidelity. To leave out the intricacies of navigating through a difficult marriage for the better part of a decade would be to ignore the biggest lessons I've learned over the course of my life to date. I also felt a moral responsibility to tell my story in its entirety, even the dark and messy parts, in hopes that it might help remove the stigma around infidelity.

Infidelity is still a relatively taboo subject, and those who are victims of it often experience an overwhelming amount of shame. Believing that they are responsible and that it is a reflection on them that their partner chose to cheat. (Note that I say "chose" because it is a conscious decision.) By staying quiet about infidelity, we perpetuate these beliefs. If you've been in a similar situation, I can tell you: it wasn't your fault. Yes, we all need to own our role in our relationships, and take responsibility for our actions and how we showed up, but there is nothing that justifies cheating and betrayal. You didn't deserve it, and you didn't bring it upon yourself.

I don't believe that a marriage that ends due to infidelity is a failure. On the contrary, I consider my marriage to have been a success. It brought me to where I needed to go and showed me the lessons I needed to learn. Then it ended. It was an issue-based relationship, what *A Course In Miracles* would call a "special relationship." It was meant to trigger both of our wounds and issues so that we could learn and heal from each other. It took ten years to do so because of my own resistance to the work and healing that needed to be done. In this type of issue-based relationship, in which we both believed our narratives about our unworthiness and unlovability, my ex-husband took on the role of the saboteur, while I took on the role of the caretaker and nurturer trying to love myself through loving someone else.

Every relationship has a reason and a season. We often experience suffering and pain when we try and take a reason-/issue-based relationship and turn it into something longer. Not everyone is meant to walk our journey with us; some show up only briefly to allow us to heal a specific wound, or to facilitate and encourage our growth.

The truth is my ex-husband was my greatest teacher and biggest healer. Because, despite my stubbornness and my strong belief about my unlovability and unworthiness, he forced me to look at my wounds and change those belief systems. I thank him for that. There is no need to demonize him or make him out to be a horrible person because he too was working through his issues with self-worth using the tools and mechanisms he knew and was familiar with.

WE CHANGE OUR BEHAVIOR WHEN THE PAIN OF STAYING THE SAME BECOMES GREATER THAN THE PAIN OF CHANGING. CONSEQUENCES GIVE US THE PAIN THAT MOTIVATES US TO CHANGE.
—DR. HENRY CLOUD & DR. JOHN TOWNSEND

My ex allowed me to look deep within myself and reconnect to my light and purpose. He showed me the type of life I was truly capable of living. And that was the greatest gift. Through our relationship and its dismantling, I found myself and therefore my salvation. That is why I now know he was my biggest healer and teacher, and I can thank him for the role he played in my life and our time together.

THE BIGGEST BETRAYAL

The person who betrayed me the most was me. That's why it hurt so much. When we take on the role of the caretaker, we try to love ourselves through loving others or try to change others through our love because we fall in love with the fantasy and the potential of who they could be. This leads us to make a lot of compromises, but these are not true compromises; they are self-betrayals. It's not the transgressions of others that most hurt; it's the transgressions that we commit against ourselves in service of others that hurt.

Until we are ready to love ourselves into fullness, we will always abandon ourselves in service of others. The world around us is a giant mirror, constantly reflecting back the parts of ourselves that still need healing or the relationships from our past that we're dragging into the present even as we try to redeem ourselves through someone new. When we treat ourselves with so much disregard, compromising our values and truths, the world around us will follow suit. No one will ever honor and love you more than YOU. You create the narrative of who you are, and that means you have the power to change it.

FIGHTING FIRE WITH WATER

This may be one of the hardest concepts to grasp because we have been taught to meet push with push and fight fire with fire. But you cannot put out a fire with more fire. Instead, you have to flood it with its opposite, water, or starve it of its fuel, oxygen. The same is true for hate and hurtful acts. We can't extinguish hate with more hate, but we can flood it with love and empathy. Hate is fueled by fear and a lack of compassion—both self-compassion and compassion for others. We can starve it of fear and lack by feeding it compassion, just as we can dissolve darkness by flooding it with light.

Part of the work of becoming a Light Warrior is to change our response pattern when we are met with resistance and negativity. Sometimes the most loving responses are setting boundaries and choosing not to engage in the fight. It may be a matter of walking away and sending love from a distance. We resist compassion out of fear that it renders us vulnerable. But the opposite is true: our foothold and stance is never stronger than when it is rooted in love and compassion. When we choose love and compassion, we align ourselves with something bigger.

INNATE WISDOM & EGO

An innate wisdom resides within each of us. We don't gather it or develop it over time; we're born with it. We instinctively know what is good for us and what isn't. Some call this our intuition.

> **INNOCENCE IS WISDOM BECAUSE IT IS UNAWARE OF EVIL, AND EVIL DOES NOT EXIST. [...] ONLY WHAT GOD CREATES OR WHAT YOU CREATE WITH THE SAME WILL HAS ANY REAL EXISTENCE. THIS, THEN, IS ALL THE INNOCENT CAN SEE. THEY DO NOT SUFFER FROM DISTORTED PERCEPTION.**
> —*A COURSE IN MIRACLES*

There is a voice deep within us, guiding us softly and gently should we choose to listen. It is often drowned out by the noise of the ego. He who speaks louder is he who is fighting to be heard: this is the truth of the ego. It is loud and relentless because that which it speaks isn't truth; we only come to believe its stories because of their pervasiveness and the fear of danger and pain. But the great weakness of the ego is that it has no power in the present. It pulls its strength from the experiences of the past and the prospects of the future; in the present moment, it can be silenced if we choose to ignore it. When we choose stillness, we can hear the voice of our inner guide and the soft and gentle voice of the Universe guiding us and showing us that it was there all along. It tells us, "You just went somewhere where I could not reach you. You were reliving the pain of the past or fearing the pain of the future, but you weren't here: living in the present."

When we succumb to the deafening voice and madness of the ego, choosing to live in the past and future, our lives ultimately erupt in chaos. Imagine yourself at the edge of a river, standing on a dock with a boat tied to it. Living under the influence of the ego is like untying the boat and placing one foot in it while keeping the other on the dock. As the current pulls the boat away, you become stretched and are forced to strain to keep your footing on the dock while not being pulled into the water. This quickly causes you to become frantic. You feel afraid of falling into the water, afraid that the boat will float away if you let go, and afraid that you will end up lost or unable to find your way back if you instead step off the dock and into the boat. This is the state of suffering perpetuated by the ego: grasping onto the past while being pulled into the future—because time never stops moving—but not being present in either in the midst of your struggle. What was no longer is, while what is to be has not yet come. But the truth is that all that really exists is the here and now. When we fear what isn't real, we rob ourselves of living in the present moment where only truth and love are real.

NO ONE WHO LIVES IN FEAR IS REALLY ALIVE.

Spiritual practice is the only thing that can keep us grounded within the present moment. It puts us in communion with our inner guide and the innate wisdom that resides within. Without a spiritual practice, our chaotic lives eventually turn to crisis. But even these crises serve a purpose. They bring us to our awakening, showing us that we are living in a world of illusion designed by the ego and our fear-based thoughts. Neither here nor there, but somewhere in between. Crises show us the illusions we've built and the dismantling required. They let things crumble so that something new can be erected. Our illusions needed to be shattered so we can see the truth. Sometimes this will come in the form of a divorce or the end of a relationship, an act of infidelity, the end of a career, or a diagnosis.

Crises brings us back to the light, so we can dismantle our illusions and old stories, burning everything to the ground so we can start anew. Moving towards the things that scare us is how we take back our power.

SPIRITUAL TESTS & CHOICES

I choose to believe that we are never being tested by an outside force. Challenges are sent to show us where work is still required and healing still needs to occur. I believe we live in a kind and compassionate Universe and, while it may not always seem like it, the events and situations that transpire happen for us, not to us. They serve our awakening and the elevation of our society. There is always more work to be done; don't fear the journey because it is the only thing that will bring you back home to yourself.

We have chosen to walk this path. As we travel it, anything of importance and truth will remain; anything useless and unreal will disappear. Your growth will trigger the growth of others, even if your life might ultimately no longer accommodate them. They may tell you you've changed, and that's ok. You have.

There are moments when we delay choosing out of fear of making the wrong decisions. We believe that it is safer to allow others to choose for us. But delegating our future to the hands of others will often bring forth chaos and crisis. If you are having trouble choosing, choose stillness. We will never have all the answers or information to know the outcomes of our choices, but in our stillness, we can tap into our inner wisdom in order to be shown the paths available to us.

TOLERANCE VS ACCEPTANCE

Most religions and organizations preach tolerance of others and their differences. But tolerance can be detrimental to our well-being and growth, keeping us on edge and guarded. Tolerating things that irritate us greatly can cause us discomfort and erode true empathy. Tolerance is based on the principle that we are different and therefore separate from one another. Instead of tolerance, let's practice acceptance. Acceptance requires that we move and get closer to each other, so close that our differences dissolve. Instead of seeing the ways we are different, we see the ways in which we are the same. Acceptance shows us that our humanity connects us and that we all want and need the same basic things: love, connection, hope, faith, belonging. These are as basic as shelter, protection, and access to clean food and water.

Let's look deeper for all the ways in which we are the same. Our souls all have the same shape. If we believe we are separate from one another, our beliefs and opinions remain unthreatened. Tolerance keeps us separate and divided, but we can all coexist without compromising or betraying our individual truths. We can understand that something we believe to be true may not be true for someone else. There is enough room for all of us and all our beliefs to coexist. When we choose to accept each other as we are, we close the gaps between us and recognize our shared humanity. In this way, we can bring about lasting change.

#LIGHT TALK & FORGIVENESS

Forgiveness is an underlying thread in most of the major religions and the foundation of all spiritual practice. It is what sets us on the path to self-actualization and personal growth. Forgiveness takes place the moment we choose—because it is a choice to forgive and to enter the present moment without the weight of our past experiences. *A Course In Miracles* says that in those moments we are born again because we are able to see for the first time without lenses tinted by our past.

> **ATONEMENT IS THE DEVICE BY WHICH YOU CAN FREE YOURSELF FROM THE PAST AS YOU GO AHEAD. IT UNDOES YOUR PAST ERRORS, THUS MAKING IT UNNECESSARY FOR YOU TO KEEP RETRACING YOUR STEPS WITHOUT ADVANCING TO YOUR RETURN.**
> —*A COURSE IN MIRACLES*

Forgiveness has been a large part of my journey and practice, and it has also been at the center of the work I do with others. When we practice empathy and extend compassion, we can bestow forgiveness onto others as well as ourselves. It is important to recognize that we're all doing the best we can with the tools we have at our disposal. Most of us were never taught how to process our emotions or the challenges that life brings. How often have we heard the words, "this too shall pass"? This implies that if you're going through something difficult or painful, just hold on because it will go away naturally with time. But this is incorrect. It is not the passing of time that heals us; it is our propensity to do the work. Those who don't know this, because they were never taught, often distract themselves from their pain through numbing or by deflecting it onto others.

We can start practicing empathy and compassion by recognizing that those who hurt us are doing so out of a lack of insight into how to process their own pain. This doesn't mean we need to forget what they've done. It certainly doesn't mean that the way we were treated is ok or acceptable. But we can put these actions and decisions into context by simply acknowledging them for what they are: the products of a survival instinct of someone who is suffering because they haven't been shown that there is another way.

BURN LETTERS

Once we've made the decision to forgive, and we've practiced bestowing that forgiveness, we get to establish boundaries. We get to decide where they lie and what space people get to occupy within our lives. Some will be sent love from a distance, others will be let in a little closer, while others may find a new place in your heart, one you hadn't imagined existed. The point is, after you've done the work, you get to decide.

One of my favorite practices is the writing of burn letters, and so I'll end this chapter with that. A burn letter is a letter from your soul, either to yourself or to another person. It's a way of letting out all that you've been holding onto and acknowledging all that you have been through and where you've come from. The beauty of a burn letter is that it never gets sent. It isn't typed or saved. It gets burned. If you can't safely burn one, I recommend shredding it or dousing it with water to let the water wash away the ink.

What goes into a burn letter? Everything and anything, but here are some prompts.

What dreams are you ready to let go of? Dreams, goals, aspirations, they're all good. They allow us to set our sights on the future and strive for something better, but sometimes they aren't ours; we inherit them from our parents and our partners, and from society. Which ones have become heavy? Which ones are keeping you stuck?

What fantasies need to die? You may be holding on to fantasies of who you could have or should have been, or fantasies of who your partner could have been, and what you could have created together. What ideals are you ready to let go of? These might be ideals of yourself, others, or society. It's time to mourn them, to hold a wake in their honor, and to release them.

Grab a pen and piece of paper, and begin to write. Address it to whomever you like, or to no one at all. Allow yourself the space to uninhibitedly express your thoughts and emotions. No judgment; no one will ever set eyes on this letter. Create an environment that works for you. It may include meditation music and some candles, or perhaps a bottle of wine, pieces of dark chocolate, and a box of tissues. Maybe you want to put on pajamas and fuzzy slippers while you blast rock and roll on the stereo. Whatever your jam, whatever feels right, just go with it.

As you write your letter, here are a few more sentence prompts to get you started and get your juices flowing.

I'm saying goodbye to this/you because... I'm leaving this situation because... I'm choosing to walk away because...

I thank you for... I'm grateful for... What I learned about myself is...

I forgive you for...

I forgive myself...

I'm ready to release...

Once you are done, it's time to burn your letter. Find a firesafe container, always. An empty kitchen sink or ashtray usually works well; just be sure to crack a window if you're doing this indoors. If you've got a fireplace, throw it in. If you're feeling any resistance, know that this is normal. When we pour so much of ourselves into something, there is an overwhelming desire to keep it and hold onto it. Maybe there was something that came out of your writing that was particularly poetic. Trust that, if it was meant to serve a greater purpose, you still have it inside of you. Our past, no matter how heavy and painful, can feel comfortable. The unknown of what comes next, once we no longer have our stories to cling to, can be frightening. But if you were compelled to write it down, then deep down you're ready to release it.

Now let it burn and release it as it goes up in flames. As it turns to ash, let it go and make room for new possibilities. If tears come, let them flow. Some dreams are heavy and need to be mourned. Others will offer a bittersweet sense of release. If you want to dance around in your underwear while sending them off into the ether, go for it. If you've got more than one letter to burn, light 'em up. Make it an annual ritual. Or a monthly one, or a daily one. If it will help you let it go, go for it. Feel the sweet sense of release.

THERE

IS A

LIGHT

THAT

NEVER

GOES OUT.

CHAPTER 12

LIGHT WARRIOR

> KNOWING OTHERS IS INTELLIGENCE;
> KNOWING YOURSELF IS TRUE WISDOM.
> MASTERING OTHERS IS STRENGTH;
> MASTERING YOURSELF IS TRUE POWER.
> — LAO TZU, *TAO TE CHING*

RISE ABOVE YOUR THOUGHTS

In the summer of 2018, I was on bed rest recovering from surgery. A minor surgery that should have had me up and at it in three days put me out for about seven weeks. I was unable to walk, stand, or sit for long periods of time. I lived my life horizontally.

It was yet another lesson and reminder of the number of things I cannot control. I had planned my goals and objectives for the year the previous December, and now, five months into the year, everything was beginning to unravel. All the projects I had planned for the summer and the second part of the year had to be put on hold. God and the Universe clearly had other plans for me.

Before my surgery, I had been racing through the months, trying to get as much done as possible, doing a million things at once. I had no plans of stopping or slowing down. I was on a mission. Not to take over the world or anything like that, but I was trying to get my work out to as many different outlets and forms of media as possible so I could help as many people as possible. It was a relentless cycle. I'd push myself for months on end, hustling through the nights and weekends, until I would ultimately burn myself out. Then I'd take a weekend off, spend it on the couch watching Netflix, and be back to the grind on Monday morning. There was no semblance of balance in my life. I had heard others say that work-life balance was just a myth, so I thought I was fine. I told myself this is what it meant to be an entrepreneur.

In early March, I had met with a surgeon about the removal of a cyst on my lower back. I had had it for about eight years and, multiple times per year, it would flare up and become infected, forcing me to take prescription antibiotics. After a few years of this, I had stopped taking the antibiotics. I was tired of them continuously wiping out my immune system, which in turn led to other health issues. It was time to find another solution. The surgeon took a quick look and concluded that it was a simple operation. I'd be in and out the same day and may need a couple days at home to recover if I felt it was necessary. I was told I would have an open wound for a while and would need to have the bandages changed daily at the local clinic. The idea of an open wound made my stomach turn and my chest tighten; I faint at the slightest sight of blood but, thankfully, the wound would be on my lower back, out of sight. I scheduled the surgery for late May so that it would be warm enough that I could wear less and looser clothing while I recovered. The timing was perfect. I'd be in and out right before the start of the summer. While I probably wouldn't be able to swim for the majority of the summer, I'd have some downtime to write and complete some projects. I booked a couple of days off following the surgery and planned to be back in the office the following Monday.

But nothing went as planned. As the anesthesia was administered, I felt consciousness slipping away and disconnected from what was going on in the operating room. I woke up hours later with a foot-long bandage that covered the bottom half of my back.

Upon opening me up, the doctors had realized the mass was significantly bigger than they had anticipated. Had I waited any longer I would have the run the risk of it becoming rooted and entangled in my spinal cord. They had managed to remove it, but the result was an open wound about six inches long, two inches wide, and two inches deep. They told me it would take at least four months to heal.

I was released from the hospital the same day, after being forced out of bed every 20 minutes so that my legs would unfreeze and I could regain my mobility. On the drive home that afternoon, the seat of the car, as well as the back of my clothes, became drenched with blood. The bleeding continued into the evening, penetrating every fabric I wore and causing my color to fade, forcing me to return to the emergency room where I spent most of the night. They managed to stop the hemorrhaging. I returned home in the early hours of the morning, freshly bandaged and with a mandate for bedrest to prevent me from popping another blood vessel and beginning to hemorrhage again. The doctors said the wound was too big and too deep; mobility posed too high a risk.

My mobility was reduced to the point that I could only stand for short periods at a time; sitting in a traditional straight-backed chair was completely out of the question. The only position I could comfortably endure was that of Sukhasana (Easy Pose): sitting cross-legged on my meditation pillow with my back unsupported, and even then, for only a few moments at a time. And so, this is what I did. I sat every morning and meditated, filling myself with light to deepen my spiritual practice during a time when I was unable to do anything else.

As I sat, I would envision a stream of brilliant white light pouring down from the sky and into my heart. With every exhale, I envisioned the ball of white light in my heart growing larger and glowing out into the room like something out of a Harry Potter movie. More streams of light would descend into my body and the light at the center of my being would grow larger and larger, filling the room and completely surrounding me until all that was left was light. As I sat marinating in that light, I would repeat the following mantra to myself, one that I learned from Gabrielle Bernstein.

> I am a Light Worker
> I am a Teacher
> I am a Leader
> I am here to spread Love
> I am here to Transform
> I am here to create great change
> I am a Light Worker

Over the course of the next few days, something miraculous began to happen. When I went to the clinic each day for my regular bandage change, I observed puzzled looks on the nurses' faces as they measured and remeasured my wound, picking back up my chart and gazing at it in confusion. The wound was healing at a rate they had never seen before, reducing by half its size from one day to the next. The original prognosis of four months of healing was quickly revised; in reality, it took only a few weeks.

For the first time, I realized just how powerful our minds are. I finally understood what Eckhart Tolle meant by "rising above our thoughts, and not below them." I could have chosen to wallow in misery about how nothing had gone according to plan and how my summer would be ruined but, instead, I chose to use this as an opportunity to focus on a different part of my being. I decided to strengthen my connection to my Source and embody the light that I was here to spread. I chose to use this time to rise above my situation and focus on my purpose. The light I called down every day was meant to bring clarity and guide me on my path. I never anticipated the healing effects it would have on my body. But, during those quiet moments as I sat on the floor with the morning sun washing over my face, I was whole. Thoughts of healing and recovery never entered my mind. In my mind, the healing had already taken place as I watched my plans and dreams unfold before me. So my body accelerated its repair to catch up.

LOOK FOR INNOCENCE IN OTHERS

I have been fortunate in my work to be able to guide others on different legs of their journey. What I have often found is that the areas where we are stuck are usually related to an experience we have remained attached to, which keeps us anchored to past moments of betrayal and reliving patterns of hurt. The deepest betrayals, aside from the ones we commit against ourselves, are usually the betrayals of those closest to us. Those wounds cut deeper than those resulting from fleeting interactions with acquaintances. But they also put us in the unique situation of being able to relate to or understand the pain of others.

I worked with a young woman named Mary who had been estranged from her older sister for years. Mary had come to the realization in her late twenties that she was attracted to other women, causing her to end a long-term relationship with a man. Her older sister ridiculed her, called her names, and treated her horribly, proclaiming that she was everything that was wrong with the world. They severed ties, and each went their separate way, but Mary always carried the weight of that experience with her. As we began to work together, Mary decided she was ready to release the past and let go of that experience and how she saw herself as a result of it. A few weeks later, when I saw Mary again, I could see that something was weighing on her. She had received a call from her mother just a few days prior letting her know that her older sister would be joining them for Thanksgiving dinner and bringing her new girlfriend with her. Mary was torn apart. All of her pain came rushing back as she sat before me. I couldn't help but smile as Mary recounted her phone conversation with her mother because she had just been given a beautiful opportunity to practice forgiveness and heal these old wounds. Mary recalled how hard it was to come to the realization that she was not only in the wrong relationship but that she had been denying a part of her identity for years. She vividly remembered what that internal struggle felt like. In an instant, she understood how painful it must have been for her older sister to watch her assume a new identity, one that was authentic to her truth, when she herself had been running from the same thing and denying who she was. She was now able to see the innocence within her sister and how her pain had twisted her actions and words as she struggled with her own identity. In that moment, she was able to extend compassion to her older sister, forgiving her and releasing herself from the burden she had been carrying. She now had the opportunity to decide whether she would rebuild that relationship and, if so, where its boundaries would lie. And she had the tools to ensure those boundaries would be based on self-love and self-respect.

Often the pain inflicted upon us is the result of another person's internal crisis or the pain they don't know how to process. When we understand that, we can recognize the struggle of others and glimpse their innocence: the wounded parts within them, the scared child, that they don't know how to deal with so instead they attempt to relieve their pain by discharging it onto others. We do not have to accept that pain or mistreatment, but we can extend compassion and practice forgiveness.

> **IF YOUR COMPASSION DOESN'T INCLUDE YOURSELF, IT IS INCOMPLETE.**
> —BUDDHA

Once we have seen the innocence in others, we see it in ourselves as well. This allows us to let go of the burdens we may be carrying and practice self-compassion and self-forgiveness.

OUR PATH & TRIBE

I didn't arrive on this Earth, in this life, or in this body with a road map declaring what my purpose would be. I had to choose to use my hardships as a vessel for growth and change, and as an opportunity to help others on their journey. That is the path of the Light Warrior. I often questioned my path and purpose, and still do to this day, wondering who am I to do this work. But that is precisely why we are Warriors—because we question ourselves and the path before us, knowing that nothing is certain, and that only through questioning can we make a choice.

> **ALTHOUGH I HAVE BEEN THROUGH ALL THAT I HAVE, I DO NOT REGRET THE MANY HARDSHIPS I MET, BECAUSE IT WAS THEY WHO BROUGHT ME TO THE PLACE I WISHED TO REACH. NOW ALL I HAVE IS THIS SWORD AND I GIVE IT TO WHOEVER WISHES TO CONTINUE HIS PILGRIMAGE. I CARRY WITH ME THE MARKS AND SCARS OF BATTLES—THEY ARE THE WITNESSES OF WHAT I HAVE SUFFERED AND THE REWARDS OF WHAT I CONQUERED. [...] THERE WAS A TIME WHERE I USED TO LISTEN TO TALES OF BRAVERY. THERE WAS A TIME WHEN I LIVED ONLY BECAUSE I NEEDED TO LIVE. BUT NOW I LIVE BECAUSE I AM A WARRIOR AND BECAUSE I WISH ONE DAY TO BE IN THE COMPANY OF HIM FOR WHO I HAVE FOUGHT TO SO HARD.**
> — JOHN BUNYAN

The path of the Warrior isn't an easy one, but it is one we choose of our own volition. It is honest and true and brings us closer to our center, our truth, and ourselves. The challenges we face show us the parts of ourselves that are wounded or incomplete, and teach us how to find wholeness in and of ourselves.

The lessons are many, but there are only three tools: faith, hope, and love. With them we can go to the deepest depths of ourselves, face tsunamis of sadness and despair, all the while knowing it will be ok and that we are held. Our path blazes the trail for those who walk beside us, our fellow Warriors, whether they realize that's what they are or not. *A Course In Miracles* teaches that we will all be brought to the same lessons and exposed to the same curriculum; only the time we choose to dedicate to learning and growing is optional.

TO BE FULLY SEEN BY SOMEBODY, THEN, AND BE LOVED ANYHOW—THIS IS A HUMAN OFFERING THAT CAN BORDER ON MIRACULOUS.
— ELIZABETH GILBERT, *COMMITTED: A SKEPTIC MAKES PEACE WITH MARRIAGE*

Through this work, we shed the masks and illusions of who we perceived ourselves to be and find our truth. We expose our authentic selves to the world, inspiring others to strip away the layers and do the same. We become beacons of light, connecting to each other to illuminate the world and dissolve the illusion that we are separate from one another. We dispense with the fear that plagues our collective consciousness.

THERE IS A LIGHT THAT NEVER GOES OUT.

As we walk this path, taking back our power and reclaiming our worth, we will attract to us other sparks of light. Divine souls who are also on this journey. They will become our tribe, our soul brothers and sisters, and spiritual running buddies. On the days when the ego taints our mind and decisions, they will be our sounding boards. On our darkest days, when we are blind to our own light, we will lean on them and their light will reflect back to us and remind us who we are.

These are our people. Cherish them, always.

#LIGHTTALK

I end this chapter with the Light Warrior Meditation. This meditation has become part of my daily practice. It allows me to extend gratitude and love to those around me and raises my vibrations so that I am showing up as the best version of myself. The prayer has become a favorite of mine, and I resort to it often when I'm feeling challenged or stuck, or when my anxiety begins to take hold and I find myself falling victim to the mad ideas of the ego. I've even recited it while driving. You may wish to do the same. Just be sure to keep your eyes open.

LIGHT WARRIOR MEDITATION & PRAYER

> Sit quietly on the floor in Sukhasana (Easy Pose) or with your legs crossed, or in a chair with your back straight and your feet firmly planted on the floor. Rest your hands on your knees or thighs, palms facing upwards.
>
> Close your eyes and begin to breathe slowly and deeply. Allow the pace of your breath to slowly bring you into a state of stillness and quiet your mind.
>
> On an inhale, envision a stream of brilliant white light descending into your body and, on the exhale, see that light extending outward from your heart and into the room. With each inhalation, more light enters your body and, on each exhalation, it extends outwards from your heart, filling the room.
>
> This light grows larger and larger and begins to surround you now. It grows brighter and brighter until all that

remains is light. You are the light.

See that light extending beyond the room and reaching out to touch different people in your life. See it extend to those you love, as well as those you wish to send compassion and healing to, even those who you desire to forgive.

Continue to sit and bask in this light as you extend it out to the world. And, when you're ready, recite the following prayer.

> Dear God (or whatever higher power you wish to evoke),
>
> I surrender to you my doubts and fears,
> my worries and insecurities,
> my thoughts of being unworthy and not enough.
> I recognize that they are not born of love,
> and do not serve me.
>
> I place them in your hands,
> and ask that they be healed.
> That they be transformed and transmuted,
> so that I may return to a place of peace and love within myself,
> Reconnecting to the light that is within me but not of me.
>
> I pray for my friends, family, and those I love
> (feel free to specify names or call out specific individuals you feel called to pray for).
> I pray for their love, their healing,
> and their blessing.

I pray for the police officers, first responders,
firefighters, and military that keep us safe.
I pray that they be protected and safely guided
home to their loved ones.

I pray for the doctors and nurses who heal us,
who witness tragedy and loss daily.
I pray that they be held in compassion and grace.

I pray for all the children who are born this day.
I pray that they be seen, truly seen.
I pray that they be loved unconditionally and that
they be blessed.

I pray for all those who are persecuted,
regardless of their gender, race, or orientation.
I pray for their strength and their willingness
to continue showing up and allowing
themselves to be seen.
And I pray that we see them for the beautiful and
magnificent beings that they are
and love them deeply.

I pray for all those who persecute others.
I pray that their fear and hatred be dissolved
and, in their place, let only love remain.

I pray that the light of our love shines so bright
that it dissolves the ignorance and fear that
pollutes our collective consciousness.
I pray that I may be a beacon of light and love
in this world.

Tell me where you would have me go,
What you would have me do,
What you would have me say and to whom.

Amen.

When you're done, slowly allow your mind to settle back into your body, becoming aware of the chair or cushion beneath you and the room around you.

Slowly wiggle your fingers and toes, bringing movement back into your body, and when you're ready, open your eyes to the room.

WE ARE THE LIGHT WARRIORS.

MANIFESTO OF THE LIGHT WARRIORS

We recognize the light as a presence within us, all of us.
It is the fiber that connects us,
and through it we find our shared humanity.

We will stumble and fall.
We will make mistakes,
and some days we will wonder what it's all for.
But in the simplest of moments,
encountering the smile of a child,
the sun shining through the trees,
we remember our center.

Some days we will question the Warrior within.
We'll question our path and purpose.
And it is precisely because we question
that we are Warriors.
We see fear as our compass,
and our hearts as our True North.

We recognize all definitions of love and light
as one and the same,
despite the labels associated with them.
We embrace all of who we are,
our faults and jagged edges,
as well as the polished and pretty parts.
Because it is the intricacies and sum of these parts
that create the unique expression
that we are here to share with the world.

We speak bravely, even when our voice quivers,
and stand against injustice.
We fight for love, equality, our planet,
and more importantly each other.

We recognize that that which is not love
is a call for love.
We practice forgiveness
and refuse to run from pain or hardship.
We know that our worth is inherent
and that our light is within us but not of us.
The divine spark that lies within us is our power,
our way home.
It cannot be altered, and it cannot be diminished.

This is our path, and this is our journey.
We are beacons of love and light. Defenders of it.
We seek it, embody it, spread it, and fight for it.
We are the Light Warriors.

AWAKENING THE **LIGHT WARRIOR** WITHIN

OUR TRIBE

IS OUR

HOME.

FIND YOUR

PEOPLE AND CHERISH THEM, ALWAYS.

ACKNOWLEDGMENTS

To my parents, who gave me the space and strength to grow as I walked this path. I know the heaviness you feel for the pain I experienced and the burdens I have carried. But know that they weren't yours to carry. This journey was a one-man excursion into the depths of my being, and the only way I could make it there and back was with the love and support you both provided me. Because of your belief in me, I knew there were no obstacles so big that I could not surmount them.

To my soul sister and spiritual running buddy Lara, for being my sounding board, my mirror, and often the voice of reason and logic. This journey would have been impossible without you, and I wouldn't be the person I am today without your presence in my life. To Mario and Jami, for being family. For giving me the privilege to have your family be part of my own, for sharing in meals together, and for your patience and understanding when game night became therapy night around the dining room table.

To my family and friends, for creating the container in which I could grow and explore the man who I was meant to become. I love you all deeply, and our time together means everything to me. Even if time and words were infinite, I could never express the depths of gratitude I hold for each of you in my heart.

To my beautiful friends Tana and Luisa. The night we spent together in NYC is among my favorite and most cherished memories. To Tana for being the voice of truth over the years and keeping me anchored to myself and what was real. I love you so much and am so grateful for the weird twist of faith that brought you into my life.

To my ex-husband and all the men I've loved before. You brought me to a better version of myself and showed me the life I was capable of living and, for that, I am eternally grateful.

To my mentors Gabrielle Bernstein, Danielle Laporte, Marianne Williamson, and Brené Brown. I know you only through the pages in your books, but your words held me and carried me through some of my darkest moments. My hope is that I can pay it forward and someday my words can help others the way yours helped me.

To Kathryn, my amazing editor. The first person to read these words and know the depths of my secrets and struggles. Thank you for your guidance; your cues and prompts made this book better than I could have imagined.

NOTES

NOTES

NOTES

NOTES

www.ingramcontent.com/pod-product-compliance
Lightning Source LLC
Chambersburg PA
CBHW030112240426
43673CB00002B/49